STARS IN KHAKI

STARS IN KHAKI

Movie Actors in the Army and the Air Services

James E. Wise, Jr., and Paul W. Wilderson III

NAVAL INSTITUTE PRESS
Annapolis, Maryland

Naval Institute Press
291 Wood Road
Annapolis, MD 21402

Library of Congress Cataloging-in-Publication Data
Wise, James E., 1930–
    Stars in khaki : movie actors in the Army and the Air services /
James E. Wise, Jr., and Paul W. Wilderson III.
      p.   cm.
    Includes bibliographical references and index.
    ISBN 1-55750-958-1 (alk. paper)
    1. Actors as soldiers. 2. Motion picture actors and actresses—
United States—Biography. I. Wilderson, Paul W., 1943– .
    II. Title.
PN1998.2.W554   2000
791.43'028'092273—dc21
[B]   00-030572

Printed in the United States of America on acid-free paper ♾

07 06 05 04 03 02 01 00   9 8 7 6 5 4 3 2
First printing

For Jim's sister and her husband, Joanell and Harry,
and for Paul's father, Paul W. Wilderson, Jr., Captain,
U.S. Army Reserve, B Battery Commander,
56th Field Artillery, 8th Infantry Division,
European Theater of Operations, June 1944–June 1945;
and mother, Helen Wilderson,
who held the family together at home

Contents

Preface

Stars in Khaki completes our trilogy of books about movie stars and entertainers who served in the military services of the United States during World War I, World War II, the Korean War, and the Vietnam conflict.

The venture has been both informative and enjoyable. We have found many of the stars and the families of others very hospitable and highly cooperative in discussing their wartime experiences or those of their late loved ones. In general these actors were proud of their service to their country and the contributions they were able to make during the various wars. A large proportion said their military experience was "the only real thing they had done in their lives."

Many remembered vividly the horrors they witnessed, and some still have difficulty discussing combat experiences. All served honorably and many were highly decorated for their courage under fire.

Perhaps we have witnessed the last film stars to be called to serve their country during wartime. But those who have served America in past conflicts have left a legacy of patriotism, sacrifice, and valor.

Finally, we need to explain briefly our use of terminology in regard to the Army's air arm. In 1914 an aviation section of the Army was created in the Signal Corps. Four years later aviation was separated from the Signal Corps and in 1920 the Army Reorganization Bill created the Air Service. An act of 1926 changed the label again, as well as initiating an aggressive expansion program, to the Air Corps. That term was commonly in use until June 1941, when President Roosevelt signed into law an autonomous Army division with the name of Army Air Forces (AAF), which remained in effect through the end of World War II. A separate third service, the United States Air Force, was created by the National Security Act of 1947.

At the outbreak of the war, the term "Air Corps" was commonly in use and it continued to permeate general parlance. At the same time and as the war progressed, the designation "Air Force" became a standard part of the language, both in and out of the military. We have used these terms interchangeably to refer to the aviation component of the U.S. Army.

James E. Wise, Jr.
Paul W. Wilderson

Acknowledgments

A s with *Stars in Blue* and *Stars in the Corps,* many assisted us in collecting materials used in writing this book. We apologize to any who are not mentioned and with our sincere thanks to all, we would like to acknowledge some very special people.

Natalie Hall, our chief research assistant, once again rendered the same measure of dedication in making this book possible. We especially acknowledge her initial draft of the chapter on Elvis Presley. She undertook that task eagerly for she remains one of the "King's" biggest fans. And we would like to thank Terry Murphy for his generous support in telling the story of his famous father, Audie Murphy.

Many thanks are also extended to Jack Green; Charlton Heston; James and Janet Arness; Mrs. Gene Autry; Maxine Hansen; Larryann Willis; John Slonaker; Lt. Col. Roger Cirillo, U.S. Army (Ret.); Harry Carrey, Jr; Brigitte Kueppers; Capt. Robert A. Guentz, U.S. Air Force Reserve; Scott Baron; Susan Bacs; Bridget Madison; Frank Coghlan; Ron Mandelbaum; David McClure; Eric Smith; Dwight Messimer; Ann Webb; Frank Hantz; Sergio Hernandez; D. Menard; and Stan Smith.

PART 1

Soldiers and Airmen in Combat

Tony Bennett

For those who participated in the Vietnam War, Tony Bennett's ballad "I Left my Heart in San Francisco" became almost a new national anthem. Bennett's lyrical voice soothed the troops' loneliness and whisked them home for a few magic moments as they yearned for loved ones left behind. They could never get enough of the man and his song; it lifted spirits every new day of fighting in that foreign land. Even today, so many years later, those familiar strains bring back emotions long since forgotten. Such was the power of legendary crooner Tony Bennett, called by the late Frank Sinatra "the greatest pop singer in America."

Tony Bennett continues today to thrill audiences with his talent. Even the youth of America have discovered Bennett because of his enthusiastic acceptance of contemporary music and emerging artists. Now in his seventies, he still enjoys "The Good Life."

(Photofest)

Tony Bennett was born Anthony Dominick Benedetto on 3 August 1926 in the borough of Queens, New York. Tony's father, a tailor and grocery store owner, had a beautiful voice and passed that gift down to his two sons. Tony's older brother, John, was a member of the Metropolitan Opera's children's chorus until his voice began to change, when he gave up any serious thought of becoming a professional singer. Tony, however, loved to sing, and also to draw pictures. Those two great loves remain with him today. Though he takes great pride in his musical accomplishments, he is equally enthusiastic about his status as an acclaimed watercolor artist.

Tony studied commercial art at the High School of Industrial Art in Manhattan. While attending school he spent much of his free time going to shows and listening to many of the great artists of the day. He became one of the original Sinatra "groupies" and often would stay for as many as seven shows a day just to watch and listen to the star when he was singing with the Tommy Dorsey Band. He also studied another Dorsey band singer, Jo Stafford, as well as the Pied Pipers, Buddy Rich, Ziggy Elman, and an act by the name of Clayton, Jackson, and Durante. Years later he was to become good friends with Jimmy Durante. Tony's three all-time favorite artists are Frank Sinatra, Jimmy Durante, and Louis Armstrong.

Tony left school to seek employment at the age of sixteen. He took on various menial jobs but always kept his eye on the career he believed he was destined for—singing. He began by participating in amateur shows in clubs around Brooklyn. These shows allowed anyone to get up and perform, and let the audience decide who was the best. Bennett won many of the contests and often received a percentage of the box office. As a teenager he had found a way to make money doing the work he loved most.

When the Japanese bombed Pearl Harbor in 1941, Tony was only fifteen years old and still lost in his world of music, art, and baseball. After war was declared, however, many of his friends and relatives were called to serve in the armed forces. In 1942 his older brother was inducted into the Army Air Force and stationed in Blackpool, England. When 1944 rolled around Tony had reached the age of eighteen and was drafted into the Army.

Anthony Benedetto was shipped to Fort Dix, New Jersey, for basic training, then on to Fort Robinson in Little Rock, Arkansas, for another six weeks to become an infantry rifleman. One of his greatest surprises was the level of bigotry he experienced. Almost immediately he saw that Italians, Jews, African Americans, and other minority ethnic groups were singled out for verbal and physical abuse, something that continued throughout his tour in the Army. After completing his training he was sent home to wait to be called up. Soon he was on his way to Germany as one of thousands of replacement troops pouring onto the Continent.

The replacement soldiers disembarked at Le Havre, France, and were held in a replacement depot before being sent to the front. The eighteen- to twenty-year-old troopers were barely trained, some never having fired a weapon. The policy of both the British and the German armies was to withdraw an entire unit following heavy losses and replace them with a new group. American practice at the time was to send replacements directly to battered units to keep the pressure on the enemy. Too often the replacements could not be broken in by battle-hardened veterans because of heavy fighting and many were killed needlessly, often without firing a shot. During the last year of the war in Europe, much of the Army ground fighting was done by replacement soldiers. Sadly, many became casualties within a few days of joining their units. But the policy of continuing a steady flow of troops to the front continued.

Bennett was assigned to the Seventh Army, G Company, 255th Infantry Regiment, 63d Division. By March of 1945, following the Battle of the Bulge, he was in Germany. His unit replaced battered American soldiers who had fought in that fierce encounter. Though the Germans had retreated, more bitter fighting lay ahead before Germany would finally surrender.

G Company crossed the Rhine late in March and fought its way into Germany engaging in house-to-house combat in many small towns. On one occasion Bennett and thousands of other soldiers were pulled off the line to see a Bob Hope show. Hope's group consisted of actress Jane Russell, comedian Jerry Colonna, and Les Brown's band. The show was a huge success, and for Tony Bennett it was a highlight of the war. He experienced and later remembered how those entertainers boosted the GIs' sagging morale. Mesmerized, Tony renewed his vow to make show business his life's work. He felt that the greatest gift one could give was a laugh or a song. Bob Hope and his performers certainly did

Near the end of World War II, Tony Bennett was an infantryman attached to the 255th Regiment, which fought its way through Germany. After the war ended, Bennett was reassigned to Special Services and sang with army musical groups. Members of his regiment are shown following the 10th Armored Division into Sinsheim, Germany, in search of enemy snipers. (National Archives)

that, and in a very real way they helped America's fighting men win World War II.

Back at the front, G Company continued its drive eastward until it reached the Kocher River and established a bridgehead at Weissbach in early April. Soon they reached the Danube. The 255th's final task was to liberate prisoners incarcerated in a concentration camp near the town of Landsberg. To reach the city and the camp they had to forge the swift currents of the Lech River while under enemy fire. Once across, they quickly silenced the enemy guns and took possession of the camp.

Bennett still remembers the horrible scene that he and his comrades encountered upon entering the camp. The gaunt and starved survivors just stood and stared at the liberators wandering about the camp. They had suffered so greatly during their captivity that they could not understand that friendly soldiers had come to save them. The troops soon discovered that all the women and children in the camp had been killed as the Allied forces fought their way toward Landsberg and that half of the remaining inmates were executed only the day before. Some of the survivors were from their own 63d Division.

When Germany surrendered, Bennett expected to be sent to the Pacific to fight the Japanese. Instead, although many of the troops in Europe were returned home, Bennett, with only four months in Germany, was assigned to Special Services in the American Occupation Army. The 255th was stationed in Mosbach, and its band, which had been formed in 1943 at Camp Van Dorn in Mississippi, and later disassembled, was reestablished. Instrumentalists, singers, and entertainers of every sort were sought to travel and entertain the troops. Bennett related in his autobiography, *The Good Life,* that he joined the group only by accident. An officer heard him singing in the shower one day and suggested that he join the newly formed regiment band. Bennett auditioned and was soon reassigned. He became a mainstay with the group, working with musicians and arrangers, many who would rejoin him later in his career.

Bennett was eventually assigned to the American Forces Radio Network in Wiesbaden, Germany. When the famed Army Air Force Band (formed and led by Glenn Miller before his plane vanished in December 1944) was returned to the States after the war, the chief of Special Services ordered that a new band be created to take its place, one that was on a par with first rate pop-jazz groups that were cropping up back home. Bennett was initially assigned as librarian for the band (the 314th Army Special Services Band), but when WO Harold Lindsay "Lin" Arison (organizer of the group) heard him sing, Bennett was added to the 314th's roster as one of four vocalists.

Bennett sang with the band on a weekly radio broadcast called *It's All Yours,* similar to Glenn Miller's earlier Army Air Corps program, *I Sustain the Wings.* The new band, a favorite among the GIs, played everything from jazz to light classical music, and Bennett sang many of the songs that he later recorded. He loved the musical freedom that Arison allowed.

In August 1946 Bennett headed for home aboard the SS *Washington.* He received an honorable discharge from the Army on 15 August. At the time of his discharge he wore the combat infantryman's badge, the American Campaign Medal, the European–African–Middle Eastern Campaign Medal with campaign Bronze Stars, the World War II Victory Medal, and the Army Occupation Medal.

Using his GI Bill entitlement, Bennett enrolled at the American Theater Wing's professional school and worked at various singing jobs in his off time. The big bands were breaking up at the time, and he most often played in small New York lounges. His first big break came with a second-place finish on *Arthur Godfrey's Talent Scouts* network television show. The winner was a young female vocalist named Rosemary Clooney. The two singers became good friends and later performed on Jan Murray's television show, *Songs for Sale.* Famed entertainer Pearl Bailey saw that program and added Bennett to a revue she was headlining at the Greenwich Village Inn nightclub. Bob Hope took in the review and was so impressed with Bennett that he asked him to join his show at the Paramount Theater. Bennett, still using the name Joe Bari, later stayed with the show as it went on tour.

Hope thought Bennett could improve on his stage name and asked Bennett what his real name was. When he was told it was Anthony Dominick Benedetto, Hope thought for a minute and said, "That's too long for a theater marquee; we'll call you Tony Bennett." Hope also advised Bennett to come out on stage with a warm smile on his face to let the audience know that he liked them. Bennett took that advice to heart, and anyone who has seen him perform remembers the exuberant smile with which he greets his audience. He is one of those few performers who "captures" his audience and holds them until the last note is sung and a standing ovation ensues.

Upon hearing Bennett's version of "The Boulevard of Broken Dreams" on a demo recording, Mitch Miller, then head of Columbia Records' artist and repertoire department, signed the singer. Columbia put the number out as a single, but it was his next recording, "Because of You" (1951), that captured the public and made Tony Bennett a household name. The record remained number one on the music charts for eight weeks and sold more than a million copies. Bennett had his first gold record. His other 1951 releases, "I Won't Cry Anymore," "Blue Velvet," and "Solitaire," also reached the charts.

When Tony Bennett released "Rags to Riches" in 1953, he began a run of hit records during the decade that included "Stranger in Paradise,"

"There'll Be No Teardrops Tonight," "Cinnamon Sinner," "Just in Time," "Smile," and "Climb Every Mountain." During that period he appeared in major nightclubs in New York and Las Vegas and in 1956 was the summer replacement for Perry Como on his network television show.

Bennett went without a hit in 1960 and 1961. But in 1962, when he was booked into the Fairmont Hotel in San Francisco for the first time, he selected a song for his opening that would change his life. Written in 1954 by two unknown songwriters, "I Left My Heart in San Francisco" became an immediate and resounding hit for Bennett. He recorded the song in January and it stayed on the charts for twenty-one weeks. Bennett was honored with two Grammy Awards for Record of the Year and Best Male Vocal Performance. In two years the record sold more than one and a half million copies in the United States, and in Britain it was a best seller for eighteen weeks. "I Left My Heart in San Francisco" turned out to be the biggest hit of Tony Bennett's career. It remains a mainstay of his repertoire, and audiences around the world still love the lyrical ballad.

During the mid-1960s a number of Bennett's recordings hit the music charts, including "I Wanna Be Around," "The Good Life," "When Joanna Loved Me," "Who Can I Turn To," and "For Once in My Life." He was named Performer of the Year by *Variety* in 1964. In 1965 he appeared in his one and only movie, *The Oscar*. Critics were not kind to the film, but they gave Bennett passing grades for his performance. He had other film opportunities, but his heart was not in acting; his passions, as always, were singing and painting.

In the late 1960s the music world changed. Columbia demanded that Bennett record songs in the top forty regardless of their appeal to him. He saw that the recording industry had become increasingly market driven and now favored young rock groups. Bennett resisted changing his style and eventually had a falling out with Columbia. Yet even after leaving the company he continued to perform before packed houses. He soon turned to different labels and recorded albums of voice and piano duets. In 1979 his son Danny took over his management and with great effort eventually reconciled his father with Columbia. After nine years without a new release, Bennett made a series of recordings on compact disks. Featuring cameo appearances by famous jazz musicians, Bennett's albums received critical acclaim.

In 1992 Bennett recorded a compact disk titled *Perfectly Frank,* which featured the music of Sinatra and soon went gold. It also brought him his first Grammy Award in three decades. Bennett's career took on a new life as he began to appeal to younger listeners through different media. He sang "Capital City" on the television cartoon situation comedy *The Simpsons* in 1991, and his rendering of "Rags to Riches" was heard over the opening credits of the movie *Goodfellas* (1990). Bennett was featured in a commercial for Nike, and in 1993 the Word-Perfect computer software company sponsored him on a national tour.

But it was Bennett's connection with MTV, the youth-oriented cable network, that created a wholly new audience for him. In the spring of 1994 he appeared in *Tony Bennett Unplugged,* in which he sang many old standards and was joined by such guest performers as k. d. lang, Elvis Costello, and J. Mascis of Dinosaur Jr. In 1995 Bennett received a Lifetime Achievement Award at the World Music Awards ceremony.

Now in his seventies, Bennett continues to record and make live stage appearances around the world. With his boyish enthusiasm and infectious smile, Tony Bennett still projects a singer who loves his work and his audience. He seeks their return love by singing straight from the heart with all the warmth he can offer. Bennett is a star in every sense of the word, one who will endure long after his shadow is gone from the stage.

Bennett has been married and divorced twice, and he has two sons and two daughters. He continues to paint in his free time, and his art has been widely exhibited. A collection of his paintings, titled *Tony Bennett: What My Heart Has Seen,* was published in 1996. It is an accomplishment, he tells readers of his biography, that he is particularly proud of.

Neville Brand

N eville Brand was usually cast as a movie bad guy. He appeared tough on the screen, and he was tough in person. His first movie was *D.O.A.* (1949). His rugged features, along with a deep, gravelly voice, made him one of the leading heavies in movies during the 1950s, 1960s, and 1970s. Brand played gangster Al Capone in *The George Raft Story* (1961) and again in *The Scarface Mob* (1962). He delivered many memorable performances, such as those seen in *Stalag 17* (1953), *Birdman of Alcatraz* (1962), and *Tora, Tora, Tora* (1970). In all he appeared in more than forty motion pictures. In addition, he was a regular on the television series *Laredo* (1965–67).

Neville Brand was born in Kewanee, Illinois, on 13 August 1921. He was one of seven children of Leo Brand, a steel worker and World

(Photofest)

War I Signal Corps veteran, and Helen Milnes. With his parents, he traveled up and down the Mississippi River to wherever a bridge was under construction. Graduating from Kewanee High School six months early, where he captained the school's football team, he falsified his birth date and joined the Illinois National Guard. In March 1941 Brand enlisted in the Army. By the time he had completed infantry training, the Japanese had attacked Pearl Harbor and America was at war.

Neville Brand was a platoon sergeant assigned to Company B, 331st Infantry Regiment (the Thunderbolts). After landing at Normandy, he saw combat in France, Luxembourg, Belgium, and Germany. Members of his unit are shown moving out of Garzweiler, Germany, toward their next objective. (National Archives)

As the Army amassed troops and established units across the country in preparation for war in Europe and the Pacific, Brand was sent to Camp Carson at Colorado Springs. There he was promoted to platoon sergeant and assigned to Company B, 331st Infantry Regiment, 83d Infantry Division (the Thunderbolts).

Brand was shipped to the European theater, where he landed in Normandy early in July 1944. As a member of the 83d Division, he saw combat action in France, Luxembourg, Belgium, and Germany, fighting in the Ardennes, through the Rhineland, Westphalia, Hanover, and Saxony. On 7 April 1945 he was wounded near the Weser River.

Brand was discharged from the Army as a staff sergeant in October 1945. While fighting in Europe he received the Silver Star, a Purple Heart, the American Defense Service Medal, and the European–African–Middle Eastern Campaign Medal with three Bronze Service Stars. Neville Brand's service record, at one time held by the National Personnel Records Center in St. Louis, apparently was lost in the 12 July 1973 fire at that facility. They do not at present hold his file; the details of his military service noted here were compiled by the center using alternative record sources.

Following the war, Brand migrated to New York, where he settled in Greenwich Village. He found himself associating with actors and writers, and when he heard about the American Theater Wing he enrolled as a student, using his GI Bill entitlement. While at the school he acted in several films for the Army Signal Corps, playing opposite another struggling actor named Charlton Heston.

After two years in New York, Brand found movie acting to his liking and began to also work in Hollywood. He enrolled in the Geller Drama School in California, and he received plaudits for a strong performance in his first movie, D.O.A. Three years later he played an American prisoner-of-war, costarring with William Holden in Stalag 17. He decided to stay on the West Coast permanently and in 1954 was cast in his first leading role in Return to the Sea, the only romantic part he ever played.

Brand's role as a convict in the 1954 prison drama Riot in Cell Block 11 was his most acclaimed. He also was noted for his fine performance opposite Burt Lancaster in Birdman of Alcatraz (1962). Brand played in more than forty films over the course of his career. He also made numerous television appearances, in such shows as *The Untouchables, Laredo, The Captains and the Kings, The Seekers,* and *Evils of the Night.* In 1958 Brand won the Sylvania Award for his live television portrayal of Willie Stark in *All the King's Men.*

Neville Brand was married three times and had two daughters with his second wife. He died on 16 April 1992.

Art Carney

Best known for his brilliant comic performances as sewer worker Ed Norton in Jackie Gleason's classic 1950s television series *The Honeymooners,* for which he won five Emmy Awards, Art Carney was also an acclaimed movie actor. In fact, Gleason often asserted that it was Carney who made him a star. Both men had failed in initial nightclub appearances during the early 1940s, but Gleason changed his act and eventually found regular work on the circuit.

Art Carney was never comfortable alone on stage delivering monologues, but he was a superb mimic, and bandleader Horace Heidt with his Musical Knights added Carney to his traveling entourage. Carney was FDR one minute, Al Smith the next, then Jimmy Stewart, along with a host of other characters. When he later carried this talent to radio, the White House called the producers of the popular CBS show

(Photofest)

The March of Time and asked that Carney not be allowed to mimic FDR because it sounded as if the president were in fact appearing on the program.

Arthur William Matthew Carney was born on 4 November 1918 in Mount Vernon, New York, the youngest of six sons of Edward Michael and Helen (Farrell) Carney. Edward Carney was a newspaperman and publicist. A spirited youth, Art showed early talent as a gifted mimic, organizing and performing one-man shows in his home. He graduated from A. B. Davis High School in Mount Vernon in 1936 and shortly thereafter left home to try his hand at show business.

Art Carney married Jean Myers, his high school sweetheart, in August 1940; in September 1942 their daughter, Eileen Wilson Carney, was born. Carney now had a family, and by this time he was having some success in his chosen profession. But this also was wartime, and in May 1944 he was drafted into the Army. Two of his brothers were already in the service, one in the Navy Dental Corps, the other attached to the Army's 46th Special Service Company in Italy.

Following basic training, Carney found himself in Europe two months after the invasion of Normandy. The war was far from over, and there was still plenty of fight left in the German war machine. Carney was assigned as a replacement with Pennsylvania's Keystone Division, but eventually was attached to the 28th Infantry Division at the Viere sector in France. The 28th arrived at the end of the Normandy campaign and would see more than its share of action as the war progressed.

Carney was manning a machine-gun position at St. Lo on 15 August 1944 when a German mortar shell blew him into the air and severely wounded his right leg. He was put on a litter and evacuated from the Normandy beachhead bound in a body cast.

Carney initially was taken to an Army hospital in the English Midlands. Though doctors worked diligently to repair his leg, they were unable to set it properly. The unfortunate result for Carney was a right leg that was three-quarters of an inch shorter than the left and a limp that has stayed with him since that time.

Several months later Carney was shipped back to a military facility in the states, McGuire General Hospital near Richmond, Virginia. During a nine-month recuperation in the hospital he became the resident clown with his humorous antics and his talent for mimicry. Because he

Two months after the Normandy invasion, Art Carney was sent to Europe and assigned to the 28th Infantry Division at the Viere sector in France. While in combat he was severely wounded in the leg by a German mortar, which ended his war service. He spent nine months recovering from his wounds, thus being denied the chance to march with his division into Paris, passing through the Arc de Triomphe and down the Champs-Élysées. (National Archives)

was older than most of the men in the ward, Carney often took on a paternal role, helping the wounded young soldiers get through the trials and tribulations of their sufferings and listening to their personal problems. Carney was awarded a Purple Heart Medal and finally discharged from the hospital in April 1945.

It was just as well for Carney that he left the war when he did because his unit underwent a severe mauling in the Battle for the Hurtgen Forest just four months later. The Germans had heavily mined the forest floor, built numerous bunkers, and used artillery effectively to explode at treetop level and force the Americans to the ground, where they were met with massive machine-gun, rifle, and mortar fire. The gruesome toll was so great that the Germans referred to the Keystone shoulder patch of Carney's unit as the "Bloody Bucket of Blood." The 28th Infantry Division suffered 6,184 combat casualties and 620 cases of battle fatigue in trying to take the Hurtgen. Every man in the division was a casualty of some sort.

When Carney returned to New York, he went back to CBS radio to do some of the old shows once again, and to add a few new ones. Once more he was on the fast track. In 1946 he and Jean added a second child, Brian, to the family.

Carney's first real break came when he was tagged for *The Morey Amsterdam Show*. The radio program's format consisted of a fictionalized New York nightclub, the Golden Goose Cafe, where Amsterdam introduced a number of well-known theater celebrities. Carney was hired to play a dumb doorman and, later, Newton the Waiter, parts that allowed him to display his comic genius. New York critics took notice of Carney, and when the show ended in 1950, he joined Henry Morgan on his television program, playing the comedy role of a dumb athlete. Although Morgan was one of television's early angry men, who trashed sponsors, descended into sarcastic diatribes, and terrorized cast members, Carney got along well with him.

Art Carney made his major breakthrough in show business when Jackie Gleason signed him for his television show *Cavalcade of Stars*. One of the program's sketches, "The Honeymooners," in which Carney's character Ed Norton was born, made television history. Carney was soon a major television star. During his early days with Gleason, Carney and his wife had a second son, Paul. His five Emmys for the Gleason show came between 1953 and 1955, and in 1966 and 1967. Another Emmy came to him in 1959 for "Outstanding Program Achievement in the Field of Humor."

Carney's contract with Gleason allowed him to pursue other performing opportunities. He appeared on *Studio One, Playhouse 90, Kraft Television Theater, Lux Video Theater,* and other television specials that displayed the richness of his talents. He went on to appear in several Broadway productions, and his performance in the play *Lovers* in 1968 earned him a Tony Award nomination. Carney appeared in twenty-three motion pictures and in 1974 won the coveted Academy Award for best actor for his role in *Harry and Tonto*.

Over the course of the years Carney's marriage to Jean Myers disintegrated, and in 1966 they were divorced. Both remarried but later divorced their spouses. The two got back together in the late 1970s and remarried in 1979.

Art Carney still makes occasional appearances but now is largely retired from show business. He remains a legend in the lore of early television. Art Carney, Sid Caesar, Ernie Kovacs, Steve Allen, Jackie Gleason, Lucille Ball—all made television the dominant media that it became. And it should be remembered that those pioneering TV performers appeared live before the cameras, a difficult challenge rarely met today.

Jackie Coogan

E arly in World War II the Japanese quickly took over much of Southeast Asia, not only defeating the Americans in the Philippines but also driving the British out of Singapore, Malaya, Thailand, and Burma. By 1943, however, the Allies were ready to go back on the offensive, and British Brig. Gen. Orde Wingate undertook a campaign in Burma far behind Japanese lines to disrupt communications and destroy supply dumps. The initial success of his three thousand "Chindit" irregulars was marginal, but a few months later he picked up the support of American air commandos, who transported men and supplies into Burma in gliders. In March 1943, when C-47 aircraft towing Waco gliders lifted out of India and loosed their load behind the lines in Burma, the lead pilot, who brought his craft down safely in the landing zone, was Jackie Coogan, the famous child actor of the 1930s.

(U.S. Air Force)

Glider pilot Jackie Coogan, *front row, kneeling at right,* shown with Cochran's Air Commandos in Burma during World War II. (U.S. Air Force)

Although many actors did not get into show business until after they completed their military service, a number of them had already seen some success on the stage and the screen. There were few servicemen/actors, however, who had achieved as much and were as well known as Jackie Coogan. Coogan had been a true child star. Born John Leslie Coogan, Jr., on 24 October 1914, Jackie was the son of vaudevillians. He made his screen debut at the age of eighteen months in *Skinner's Baby;* at four years of age he became a regular in swimmer Annette Kellerman's outdoor review. Charlie Chaplin saw the act in Los Angeles and signed Coogan to appear in his first feature film, *The Kid.* The movie, with Chaplin as "the Tramp" raising a streetwise orphan, mixed slapstick and sentiment in a winning combination. Playing his part with the skill of a professional, Coogan caught the fancy of filmgoers, and he became a major star almost overnight. In fact, his career as a child star was phenomenal, and his every move was reported by the world press.

Coogan was one of the highest paid actors in Hollywood, receiving million-dollar contracts for movie appearances. On one occasion he was given half a million dollars just for switching studios. His movie career waned as he reached his teens, however, especially after his famed locks were cut when he was twelve. The trim was a news-making event. Much of the money Coogan earned as a child was kept in trust by his parents, but after his father died in an auto accident and his mother remarried, Coogan, then twenty-one and married to starlet Betty Grable, found himself unable to support his bride. Because his mother and new stepfather were reluctant to turn over his money, he sued his family in 1938. By the time the lawsuit was resolved, there remained only $252,000 in the account, half of which he received. As a result of this contentious court action, California passed a bill commonly known as the Coogan Act, which prevented such abuses. Henceforth, court-administered trust funds were set up for child actors.

Coogan appeared in few movies in the years just prior to his World War II Army Air Force service. By the time of his discharge in 1945, Flight Officer Coogan had flown twenty missions with the 1st Air Commando Group and earned an Air Medal, the American Campaign Medal, the Asiatic-Pacific Campaign Medal, and the World War II Victory Medal. After the war Coogan returned to the screen and played mainly character parts, but television proved to be his forte, and he appeared in some fourteen hundred shows. He is probably best remembered as Uncle Fester in the TV series *The Addams Family*. Coogan appeared in more than forty movies during his career.

Divorced from Betty Grable in 1939, Coogan married three more times. His younger brother, Robert Coogan, was also a movie and television actor, as is his grandson, Keith Mitchell. Jackie Coogan died in 1984.

Charles Durning

C harles Durning has always found it difficult to talk about his experience in World War II. In a 1993 interview he said, "I've only told my wife, because she demanded to know why I sobbed in my sleep." Durning was drafted in 1943, shortly before his twentieth birthday. He went on to recall "hours and hours of boredom and 10 minutes of horror that overshadow your whole life. There were 70 of us that survived that first day at Normandy, but I was the only survivor of a machine-gun ambush. I was in the first wave to hit Omaha Beach. Later I was crossing a field somewhere in Belgium. A German soldier ran toward me carrying a bayonet. He couldn't have been more than 14 or 15. Even though he was coming at me, I couldn't shoot." Durning was stabbed eight times in the arm, right shoulder, and back and was hospitalized. He was released in time to take part in the Battle of the Bulge.

(Photofest)

Charles Durning was twenty years old when he landed on Omaha Beach during the Normandy invasion. He was wounded three times and received three Purple Hearts and a Silver Star for his courageous wartime service. (Photofest)

On 16 December 1944 twenty-five German infantry and armored divisions consisting of three armies burst through the thinly held lines of exhausted American troops along a sixty-mile front from Aachen in the north to Echternach in Luxembourg. The ensuing struggle, known as the Battle of the Bulge, was the largest land campaign fought by American forces during World War II. It was to be the last major German counteroffensive of the war along the western front. Hitler believed that his "Operation Wacht am Rhein" (Watch on the Rhine) could regain the initiative and stabilize his deteriorating position in the Ardennes by splitting the Allied forces in a surprising drive to recapture Antwerp.

Other than heroic efforts to hold the line by several American units, such as the 7th Armored Division at St. Vith and the 101st Airborne at Bastogne, the sudden advance of German forces proved highly successful. The German offensive was led by General Dietrich and his Sixth Panzer Army on the main front, General Manateuffel's Fifth Panzer Army in the center, and the Seventh Army of General Brandenburger in the south, along with "Operation Grief," a German brigade disguised as American soldiers who infiltrated the American line and disrupted attempts to halt the German thrust.

Eisenhower's SHAEF (Supreme Headquarters Allied Expeditionary Forces) reacted slowly to the situation, thinking they were witnessing a local attack at Monschau. The scale of the German operation quickly made itself clear, however, and Eisenhower and his lieutenants were only able to stem the advance by throwing two hundred thousand troops into the breech during the first four days of the battle. Counterattacks by the reinforced American units, together with heavy fighter-bomber raids on German columns, halted the German drive and convinced Hitler to withdraw his troops from the decreasing bulge.

The Ardennes battle cost the Americans some 75,000 casualties (8,497 killed, 46,000 wounded, 21,000 missing or captured). Charles Durning was taken captive with about 150 other soldiers. They were forced to march through a pine forest near Malmédy, Belgium, where Durning and two companions managed to escape to the American lines. When American forces recaptured the forest, they discovered that all the prisoners had been massacred. Durning was brought along to help identify the bodies.

Not long afterward Durning was wounded in Germany. "I was shot in the chest by a bullet, a ricochet," he recalled. He was once again hospitalized, and this last wound ended his war service. Over the next four years Durning was hospitalized periodically for treatment of both his physical and his psychological wounds. "The physical injuries heal first," he noted; "it's your mind that's hard to heal."

For his valor in action against the enemy, Charles Durning was awarded the Silver Star; he also received three Purple Hearts. In 1994, on the fiftieth anniversary of D day, Durning led the commemorative ceremony at Arlington National Cemetery.

Charles Durning's early life had not been a great deal easier than his wartime experience. He was born in 1923 in Highland Falls, New York, the ninth of ten children. Five of his sisters died of disease in childhood, three of them within a period of two weeks. His father, who had been exposed to mustard gas while serving in the Army in World War I, died when Charles was twelve years old. His mother supported her five surviving children by washing cadet uniforms at the West Point laundry.

Durning dropped out of high school and left home when he was fifteen. He labored on a farm, in a munitions factory, and as a pipefitter's assistant, but found his true calling when he took a job as an usher in a burlesque house. He studied the comics' routines, and when one of them did not show up, Durning convinced the manager to give him a chance. He later remembered, "The first time I got laughs, I was hooked."

Durning's first inclination when he left the Army was to head back to the stage, but it took almost a decade for him to fully recover from his service ordeal. In order to get over a stutter he had developed, he began studying acting and modern dance. He later enrolled at the New York Academy of Dramatic Arts. Over a two-year period he gained invaluable acting experience by appearing in a different play every week at the Brooklyn Playhouse, about one hundred roles overall. Nevertheless, the school had little faith in his ability and did not encourage him to return. Durning, however, was not easily deterred, and he joined various touring groups, accepting whatever parts were available.

In 1962 Joseph Papp, the producer of the New York Shakespeare Festival in Central Park, saw Durning in an off-Broadway play and asked him to audition for the festival. Over the next eleven years Durning acted in thirty-five plays produced by Papp, but he received little notice. In 1973, however, he appeared in Papp's *That Championship Season* and garnered favorable reviews from the critics. Durning would later say that it took him sixty plays to gain the critics' attention. But that attention won him a part in the movie *The Sting,* which starred

Paul Newman and Robert Redford—a role that proved to be the beginning of an illustrious career for the fifty-year-old actor.

To date Durning has appeared in some fifty movies. He was nominated for an Oscar as best supporting actor for both *The Best Little Whorehouse in Texas* and *To Be or Not to Be*. He has been cast in numerous television shows, including the sitcom *Evening Shade*. Durning has returned often to his first love, the Broadway stage, and in 1990 he won a Tony Award for the revival of *Cat on a Hot Tin Roof*. Charles Durning is still active in the theater and recently toured with costar Julie Harris in the stage play *The Gin Game*.

Malmédy Massacre

The Battle of the Bulge was launched on 16 December 1944 when massed German forces struck the Allies along a broad front near the German border with Belgium, Luxembourg, and France. The Malmédy Massacre occurred on 17 December. Battery B, 285th Field Artillery Observation Battalion, 7th Armored Division, was en route to St. Vith when Kampfgruppe (Task Force) Peiper's leading tanks suddenly appeared from the east near Malmédy in Belgium. SS colonel Jochen Peiper was a ruthless twenty-nine-year-old veteran of the eastern front. He had under his command 110 tanks and four thousand men of the elite 1st Panzer Division Leibstandarte Adolf Hitler. Peiper's panzers drove through the American battalion firing and causing panic among the surprised GIs. Unprotected by tanks or heavy weapons, the Americans abandoned their vehicles and ran into a nearby forest to avoid the onslaught.

An American soldier gazes at the bodies of U.S. officers and soldiers discovered beneath the snow in a field at Five Points, near Malmédy, Belgium. The unarmed men were gunned down on 17 December 1944 after being taken prisoner by German soldiers during the Battle of the Bulge. (National Archives)

Peiper ordered the Americans, about 150 in all, rounded up and herded into a nearby field as a second panzer column appeared. The Germans positioned a tank at each end of the snow-covered field. A German officer in a command car stood up and killed an American medical officer in the front rank with his pistol and then shot another officer standing next to the doctor. With that, the two tanks began firing into the crowd of POWs with their machine guns. About seventy of the POWs miraculously survived the massacre by running into the forest.

The dead soldiers were discovered by an American patrol soon afterward, and news of the incident spread rapidly through the American lines. As a result many surrendering SS officers were shot, and GIs who were thinking of surrendering had a change of heart. During the first four days of the Battle of the Bulge, Peiper's troopers murdered some 350 American POWs along with many unarmed civilians.

Following the war, surviving members of the Kampfgruppe, including Peiper, were put on trial and sentenced to death, though their sentences were later commuted. Paroled in 1956, Peiper was killed in a house fire twenty years later, some say by former members of the French Resistance.

Clark Gable

"**F**rankly, my dear, I don't give a damn"—perhaps the most famous line ever delivered by a movie star. The word "damn" itself created a startled reaction; prior to World War II such language on the screen was highly unusual. Only a star of Clark Gable's stature could pull off that line, delivered in the 1939 blockbuster *Gone with the Wind*. Gable was known as the "King of Hollywood," and his popularity with movie audiences never wavered.

To this day *Gone with the Wind* remains the most popular movie ever released in America. Considering inflation and the number of tickets sold (which continues in the present at periodic screenings), it surpasses even recent screen hits. In the summer of 1939 some 56 million Americans saw *Gone with the Wind*, an exceptionally high number given the country's population of 131 million at the time—fewer than

(U.S. Air Force)

half the number of people living in the country at the opening of the twenty-first century.

By 1939 Clark Gable had appeared in forty-six films and was listed among the top ten money-making stars. In 1934 he had been awarded an Oscar as best actor for his performance in *It Happened One Night*, costarring Claudette Colbert. She won the Oscar that year for best actress.

Known as a man's man and a woman's dreamboat, the six-foot, ruggedly handsome Gable enjoyed wide box-office appeal, especially to women, which continued until the day he could no longer act. He was a modest man, warm, friendly, and, as his Army Air Force buddies called him, a "regular guy."

Clark Gable was born in Ohio in 1901 to parents of Dutch ancestry. His father was an oil contractor, and after Clark's mother died when he was seven months old he was left with his grandparents. His father eventually remarried and Clark returned home.

Gable thought he would study medicine at college, but he soon became sidetracked by a local theater company. He found himself strongly intrigued by acting, and when he was not performing in small parts he was volunteering backstage. He did find his way to Broadway, but jobs in the theater were few and far between. By 1924 Gable had migrated to Portland, Oregon, and was married to Josephine Dillon, the director of a Little Theater group.

Learning of work in Los Angeles, the couple moved south and Gable soon had a part in a silent film. But he did not feel he was right for the medium, and he returned to New York and the theater once again. Following some good reviews and buoyed by the encouragement of actor Lionel Barrymore, Gable decided to try Hollywood again and take another shot at pictures. His first role in talking films took place in 1931, and his popularity and stardom grew as the decade wore on and he proved himself a versatile actor.

Earning thirty thousand dollars a month with MGM, by 1941 Gable had achieved financial security. By that time he was divorced and had married actress Carole Lombard, who appears to have been his one true love. When World War II began, both offered their services to the White House. They were advised to continue making pictures, which was the best way they could contribute to the morale of the armed services. Lombard was intensely patriotic, and to support the war effort she immediately started a war-bond-selling tour in January 1942. Gable, still pondering his wife's suggestion that he join the Army and earn a commission, continued to make movies.

That same year Gable met a friend, Gen. Henry "Hap" Arnold, in Washington. At the time, Arnold was involved in building up the Army Air Force, which was now focused on the concept of high-altitude daylight precision strategic bombardment. The bombers had to be defended by their own gunners because Allied fighter escorts at that early stage of the war lacked the range to protect the heavily ladened planes as they closed on their targets. Various types of crew-training films were being made at the First Motion Picture Unit (formerly Hal Roach Studios) in Hollywood, and Arnold approached Gable about producing a film on aerial gunnery for recruitment purposes. Everyone wanted to be a pilot, but Gable's face would help make the essential but less attractive gunnery billet more appealing. Gable agreed to do the film, but insisted that he enlist in the AAF as a private while he underwent officer candidate training.

Two weeks after she commenced her war-bond tour, Carole Lombard was killed in a TWA DC-3 plane crash at Table Mountain outside of Las Vegas. Gable was devastated, and in his grief told the press that he was retiring from acting, selling the Encino ranch that he and Lombard had cherished, and joining the Army Air Corps. Although MGM tried to hold on to him with alluring movie scripts, the studio heads knew it was a hopeless cause and that he was determined to join the service. They supported his endeavor by arranging, with the military's approval, for his induction intelligence test and physical to be done in secrecy. They also provided for a friend, cinematographer Andrew McIntyre, to sign up and train with Gable during his service tour. McIntyre's primary job was to ward off the fans who were guaranteed to track Gable every step of the way.

On 12 August 1942, Gable and McIntyre were sworn in at the Los Angeles Federal Building. Gable told the press that he had made application to be a gunner and that he would do his very best. Only he and General Arnold knew his true assignment.

Gable reported to the Miami Air Officer's Training School. He was given a crew cut, his famous mustache was shaved, and he was issued government clothing. Assigned quarters in the Collins Park Hotel, which had been taken over by the AAF, Gable and McIntyre were soon photographed scrubbing lobby floors, just like any other soldiers.

Gable was promoted to corporal as he began officer candidate training. He and McIntyre were assigned to Class 42-E, which consisted of twenty-six hundred men, and to Squadron I. The two immersed themselves in their daily training routine, which was tough. Although he was forty-one years old at the time, Gable never complained. Classwork was easy for the actor because he had spent so many years memorizing movie scripts. He treated classwork in the same manner and passed tests easily. The long marches in the hot Florida sun were more of a problem, but he told the press that he was "enjoying Army life, had lost ten pounds, and was feeling fine." Upon graduation he ranked seven hundred in his class.

Fans continued to be a hazard for Gable. Often, when he was walking guard duty, women would throw paper missiles at him through the base fence, no doubt offering their phone numbers and perhaps other amenities. They would even attempt to get into his quarters. The Army eventually had to move his training away from public view.

Gable and McIntyre graduated from OCS as second lieutenants on 28 October 1942. General Arnold gave a speech and handed out diplomas personally. The class elected Gable to give the commencement speech, and although it was most likely crafted by others, it revealed his personal motivations and thoughts about individual discipline:

> I've worked with you, scrubbed with you, marched with you, worried with you over whether this day would ever come. The important thing, the proud thing, I've learned about us is that we are men. . . . Soon we will wear the uniforms of officers. How we look in them is not very important. How we "wear" them is a lot more important. . . . Our job is to stay on the beam until . . . in victory . . . we are given the command "Fall out."

Gable still mourned the loss of Lombard. Under his uniform he carried a small gold box that held some of her jewelry. His depression over her death never left him, and his insistence on facing every challenge while in the AAF regardless of the risk led his friends to believe he might have a "death wish" because of her. But that proved not to be the case.

Soon after graduation General Arnold asked Gable to gather a film crew and fly with the Eighth Air Force in Europe to begin making his documentary film. The Eighth was being hit hard by enemy air and ground defenses as it carried out its mission of daylight bombing. Aerial gunner replacements were in great demand. Gable and McIntyre were ordered to undergo an accelerated course at Flexible Gunnery School at Tyndall Field in Panama City, Florida, and to take photographic training at Camp Seven Mile, Fort George Wright, Spokane, Washington.

Gable grew back his mustache and replaced his ill-fitting uniforms with tailor-made clothes supplied by MGM costumers. He also found that he needed to keep a supply of uniform hats on hand because female fans would often snatch them from his head and run off. Gable and McIntyre won their aerial gunner's wings in January 1943. After completing photography training they reported to Biggs Field, Texas, where they joined the 351st Bomb Group equipped with B-17 Flying Fortresses. Gable and his "little Hollywood group" of cameramen, soundmen, script writers, and support personnel were assigned to the 508th Squadron as the bomb group moved to Pueblo, Colorado, in preparation for overseas combat duty with the Eighth Air Force. The 351st deployed to England in April 1943, at the same time both Gable and McIntyre were promoted to captain.

The German propaganda broadcaster, Lord Haw Haw, was soon on the airwaves greeting the Hollywood star. Luftwaffe chief Herman Goering offered a reward to any of his pilots who downed Gable's B-17. It was said that the star also gained the notice of Hitler. To all this unwanted attention Gable responded, "How can I hide with this face? If I ever fall into Hitler's hands the son of a bitch will put me in a cage like a big gorilla. He'd exhibit me all over Germany." He went on to declare that if his plane went down, "I'll just go with the son of a bitch."

Stationed at Polebrook in England, Gable flew his first mission on 4 May 1943 to Antwerp, Belgium, in Capt. William R. Calhoun, Jr.'s plane, *Eight Ball II*. On the flight he tried his hand at aerial gunnery, firing the radio-room gun. Gable and his staff had begun filming while they were at Pueblo and continued with their assignment at Polebrook.

Capt. Clark Gable talks to base personnel at an airfield in England after returning from a mission over Germany during World War II. (U.S. Air Force)

Gable made the men feel at ease in his company, and he was soon thought of as just a regular guy doing his duty. Although he was quartered in the officer's barracks, he ate his meals in the noncommissioned officer's mess.

The locals got used to seeing Gable motorbiking through the countryside. He also hunted on the Rothschild estate, where the base was located. On 10 July he flew his second mission, which targeted the air depot at Villacoublay. Unknown to Gable, recruitment and assignment of aerial gunners peaked in mid-1943, thus eliminating the need for his film. Unaware, he continued on, gaining new, close friendships among the men of the bomb group, who soon were calling him by his Hollywood nickname, "Pappy." He was generous with his time, playing softball and motorcycle dodge'em with the enlisted men. He often would pretend to borrow change from an airman to give the shy youngster an opportunity to meet him. When the press questioned him about his experiences, he would change the subject to talk about the men he flew with. "They are the greatest men in the world," he said, "and every one of them is doing a fine job, risking his life daily for us all."

Gable's camera crew recorded all aspects of the war that related to aerial gunners. He visited many bases and posed good-naturedly with air crews. He visited the fighter groups escorting the bombers, and he was popular with the Red Cross ladies and Special Services personnel.

There was talk that he flew only the "milk runs" (routine noncombat missions), but that was not true. He went on missions as scheduled, and on one occasion he almost became a casualty. On 12 August 1943 the 351st bombed a secondary target at Bochum, Germany. Flying in Maj. Theodore Milton's *Ain't It Gruesome,* Gable eased himself up behind the top turret gunner to get a better look at the enemy planes attacking the formation. Luftwaffe fighters made five passes, damaging eleven planes, killing one crewman, and wounding several others.

During the attack a 20-millimeter shell burst through the underside of the *Gruesome* and cut off the heel of one of Gable's boots. The shell exited the aircraft, passing within a foot of his head. When asked about the incident after the B-17 returned, Gable explained, "[I] didn't know it had happened. I didn't know anything about it until we had dropped 11 thousand feet (and could get off oxygen and look around). Only then did I see the hole in the turret." After this and other harrowing experiences, Gable decided to title his film *Combat America;* it would carry his view of the air war.

Gable's last mission took place on 23 September, when the 351st and 91st Bomb Groups went to the French port of Nantes. Unfortunately, poor weather caused the force to abort the mission, though enemy fighters attacked the aircraft formations. Knowing this would be his final flight with the group, Gable manned the .50-caliber nose gun in Lt. Col. Robert W. Burns's plane, *The Duchess.* On his return he told reporters, "I could see the German pilot's features. That guy won't be around very long if he keeps on doing that. I don't know how I missed him, though. I didn't hit a damned thing myself."

Gable flew five missions, and every one of his aircraft took hits. By September the camera crew had shot some fifty thousand feet of film. It was time to go home and edit it into a movie. Before he left England, Gable was awarded the Distinguished Flying Cross and the Air Medal.

He was embarrassed to receive the awards when he considered the dangers encountered by the many airmen who flew multiple missions.

Upon his arrival in the States, Gable reported to General Arnold that he and his crew were ready to produce their film. "Well, Clark, what was it I sent you to Europe for? I've forgotten," asked Arnold at their meeting. Gable answered, "To make a film. There was a gunner problem, sir." Gable reminded the general of his concern in October 1942 and how he had ordered Gable to produce an aerial gunner recruitment film. Arnold replied, "Oh, we've licked that." Gable was stunned. Arnold went on to say that they could do anything they wanted with the film they had shot.

Gable returned to Hollywood to finish the project. Once home, however, he was again reminded of the loss of Lombard. He also found that he missed the camaraderie of the Air Corps. After selling war bonds, filming *Show Business at War,* and pursuing a variety of other activities, he was still depressed. He began drinking, and he set off on long motorcycle jaunts. Exacerbating his situation, MGM invited him to the christening of the Liberty ship *Carole Lombard.* But there was a positive aspect to what Gable had witnessed during the war. After seeing so much destruction and death in Europe, he knew he had not been singled out for grief; there were many families in America now who were suffering the loss of loved ones, just as he had lost "Ma" (his nickname for Lombard).

Combat America proved to be the film that Gable hoped it would be. In its own special way it accurately portrayed the many moods, fears, fighting tenacity, and heroics of the men who manned the guns on the bombers that flew across Europe into the heartland of Germany. Gable hoped to get a new assignment, especially after he was promoted to major in May 1944, but when that seemed unlikely after the invasion of Normandy a month later, he requested and was granted his discharge.

Gable's first film after returning to Hollywood was the MGM production *Adventure,* costarring Greer Garson. Never a studio to miss a good publicity pitch, MGM trumpeted "Gable's Back and Garson's Got Him." Unfortunately, the movie did not fare well and seemed to set a pattern for Gable's postwar films. He was forty-six now and had put on weight. He drank excessively and his nerves appeared to be shattered. He married Lady Sylvia Ashley in 1949, a woman who greatly resembled Lombard. The union, however, lasted only a few years. In 1955 he married another Lombard look-alike, Kay Spreckels. His contract at MGM was not renewed. Although he did freelance work and was still the King to many, his career seemed to be at an end.

Gable probably did his best postwar work in the John Huston film *The Misfits,* which also starred Marilyn Monroe. The stress of the production and his insistence on doing his own stunts took their toll, and on 16 November 1960, he suffered a heart attack and died at the age of fifty-nine. He did not live to see the fine critical reviews of the movie, nor did he see his one and only child, John Clark Gable, who was born shortly after his death. He was buried in an Air Force ceremony, next to Carole Lombard. Perhaps words he spoke himself on an earlier occasion serve best as Clark Gable's eulogy: "The things a man has to have are hope and confidence in himself against odds, and sometimes he needs somebody, his pal, or his mother or his wife or God, to give him that confidence. He's got to have some inner standards worth fighting for or there won't be any way to bring him into conflict. And he must be ready to choose death before dishonor without making too much song and dance about it."

James Garner

J ames Garner is noted for his starring roles in two acclaimed television series, *Maverick* (1958–62) and *The Rockford Files* (1974–80), for which he won an Emmy. Garner has also appeared in a host of motion pictures over the years, including *Sayonara* (1957), *The Great Escape* (1963), *The Americanization of Emily* (1964), *Victor/Victoria* (1982), and *Murphy's Romance* (1985). He got his start in show business performing on stage at the urging of a boyhood friend who bought gas at the Shell service station where Garner worked in Hollywood. Paul Gregory, who started out as a soda jerk and worked his way up to theatrical producer, always felt that Garner should try acting.

The two men made contact after Garner returned from the Korean War. Gregory had Garner read for him for a part in the 1954 road company production of *The Caine Mutiny*. He was hired, not for a speak-

(Photofest)

ing role, but as one of the six silent judges. That experience, however, allowed him to observe the talents of the play's major stars: Henry Fonda, Lloyd Nolan, and John Hodiak. Garner concentrated on the acting, movement, and posture of Fonda on the stage and was most impressed by the actor's attitude and concentration. Garner has often declared, in fact, that he swiped practically all of his acting style from Henry Fonda.

While the critically acclaimed play enjoyed a run on Broadway, Garner spent his spare time attending drama classes at New York's Berghof Studio. When the show went on tour, he was offered the role of Lt. Stephen Maryk, then played by John Hodiak. Garner subsequently appeared in more than five hundred performances of the play until the road tour ended in 1955.

After *The Caine Mutiny* James Garner returned to Hollywood to seek more acting opportunities. He found bit parts in the television series *Cheyenne* and was eventually signed by Warner Brothers, where he was cast in supporting roles in numerous unmemorable films. He made his breakthrough as Marlon Brando's close friend in *Sayonara* (1957). A year later he gained his first starring role in *Darby's Rangers,* and that same year he was cast as the lead in a new western television series, *Maverick.* The program was an instant hit, and Garner was on his way to stardom.

Garner, whose surname was originally Bumgarner, was born in Norman, Oklahoma, on 7 April 1928 to Weldon and Mildred Bumgarner. One of three sons, he is part Native American, and his heritage includes early settlers of the Oklahoma Territory. His father was in the upholstery, carpeting, and carpentry business in Norman. One brother, Jack, became a professional baseball player, who at one time pitched for the Pittsburgh Pirates. Another brother, Charles, was a schoolteacher in Norman. Mildred Bumgarner died when James was six, and from then on he was raised by grandparents, aunts, and uncles. Much of Garner's youth was spent around ranch hands, and he often rode horses to school. At Norman High School he was an outstanding athlete in football, basketball, and track.

James Garner suffered from wanderlust, and he interrupted his schooling to spend a year as a merchant seaman on board a seagoing tug out of New Orleans. He then moved with his father to Los Angeles, where Weldon started a carpet contracting business. Garner attended Hollywood High School briefly before returning to Norman to finish his high school education, where he also joined the Oklahoma National Guard. Following graduation he returned to Los Angeles to work with his father, but the Korean War broke out and he became one of the original draftees in Oklahoma to be called for duty.

After basic training, Pvt. James Bumgarner was assigned to the 5th Regimental Combat Team of the 24th Division (the Victory Division) and sent to Korea. He spent fourteen months in Korea and was awarded two Purple Hearts, one for wounds received from friendly fire.

Although he did not trade fire with the enemy for more than six or seven days, they were, he recalled, "long, bad" days. On his second

James Garner was assigned to the 5th Regimental Combat Team (RCT) of the 24th Division (the Victory Division) during the Korean War. Shown here are members of the 5th RCT firing on the enemy along the Naktong River north of Taegu, 18 September 1950. Garner was awarded two Purple Hearts for wounds received during the war. (National Archives)

day in Korea, he was wounded while on patrol. Hit in the hand and face with enemy shrapnel, he went back to an aid station and started picking bits of metal from his face using a jeep mirror. An officer came up and ordered him to go inside the aid station and have his wound recorded and attended to. As a result, Garner was awarded his first Purple Heart. His second medal was earned during a much more precarious situation.

One night Garner's combat team was overrun on a ridge line by waves of Chinese ground forces. By morning only about 40 of his group of 130 were still alive. After retreating all night they joined with another unit early the next morning and watched as Navy Panther jets began air strikes against the Chinese positions. The American soldiers were elated and cheered the Navy airmen on until an AT-6 spotter plane flew over and identified Garner and his compatriots as another concentration of enemy troops.

They soon were under attack by Navy jets firing 20-millimeter rockets. Garner was hit in the back and his rifle was shattered. Rather than remain a sitting target in his foxhole, he scurried out of his position and jumped off the side of a cliff. After suffering phosphorous burns on his neck and tearing up his shoulder and both knees, he finally came to a halt one hundred feet down the hill. A South Korean soldier who also jumped down the hill was in worse shape, suffering extensive burn wounds. The burns suffered by both were the result of spraying phosphorus from the rockets fired by the Navy planes at the troops.

Climbing back up to the ridge line, Garner, with no weapon but still wearing his helmet, and the South Korean, armed with a rifle, found that they were alone. They saw no one along the ridge. Garner could not speak Korean, and the ROK soldier spoke no English, but both sensed they should move south along the ridge line in order to catch up with their unit.

The two eventually reached the valley they had occupied the day before only to come across a group of soldiers who were neither Americans nor South Koreans. The large group of idle North Korean soldiers paid little attention to the two soldiers as they passed, probably thinking the Korean, who held the rifle behind Garner, was one of them and the American was his prisoner. Six hours later, still on the move, they heard the familiar sounds of Sherman tanks approaching. The

ROK soldier immediately gave his rifle to Garner and took Garner's helmet and placed it on his own head. He positioned himself ahead of Garner, giving the appearance to the American troops that he was Garner's prisoner and thus ensuring his own safety. Garner later commented on the ROK soldier's actions, "That guy really picked up on all of it better than I did."

After recuperating from minor phosphorous burns and shoulder and knee injuries, Garner was transferred to Japan, where he worked in a base post office. During his nine months there he made some major modifications to the postal facility, which was located in a bombed-out shoe factory. At one point he needed materials to build a bar; when he did not get what he wanted, he simply did not deliver the mail to those who ignored his requests. It was not long before he had a bar stocked with the best whiskey and was regularly receiving ice from Graves Registration. Garner built a theater in the largest part of the factory, and he laid out a baseball diamond. He also had hot showers installed and provided the base with a swimming pool. He cleaned out the basement, cemented the floor, whitewashed the walls, and installed a ladder on the side of the pool. And before leaving Korea he received his second Purple Heart.

Before Garner left the Army, he took a high school equivalency test and received his diploma, plus credit for two years of college. Upon being discharged he wore the Combat Infantryman's Badge, the Purple Heart with Oak Leaf Cluster, the Korean Service Medal, the United Nations Service Medal, and the National Defense Service Medal. In June 1952 Garner rejoined his father in the carpeting business, but it was only temporary as he was soon off to Hollywood and a chance encounter with an old friend and the beginning of a theatrical career.

Garner is an actor who makes his work look easy. On both screen and stage he displays exceptional versatility, and over the years he has matured into one of America's most admired stars. Like Gene Hackman, Robert Redford, Paul Newman, and a few others of their stature, he can always be counted on to deliver a solid performance.

Tim Holt

T he Holts came from Virginia and are related by blood to the Marshalls, the Randolphs, the Picketts, and the Breckenridges. When Jack Holt, Tim Holt's father, became an actor, it was almost considered a family scandal. It had been a long-standing tradition that the males of the clan either became lawyers, like their ancestor John Marshall, chief justice of the Supreme Court, or soldiers, like another famous forebear, Civil War Confederate general George Edward Pickett.

When young Holt decided that he wanted to follow in his father's footsteps, the family was devastated. It was not long, however, before they recognized that Tim was a talented actor destined for success. Though he was the son of an actor, Tim Holt carved out his success entirely on his own.

(Photofest)

Born Charles John Holt, Jr., on 5 February 1918 in Beverly Hills, Tim completed his early education in local schools, then attended Culver Military Academy in Indiana, where he was in the cavalry and played varsity polo. While at Culver he roomed with Hal Roach, Jr., who was the captain of the football team on which Tim starred. Roach went on to become a successful director and motion picture producer. Holt graduated from the academy with honors, ranking fourteenth in a class of 115. He attended the University of California for a brief period until he decided to pursue a screen career.

Holt joined the Westwood Theater Guild and gained invaluable experience before seeking employment at Universal Studios. At first he found bit parts in low-budget films, but his break came when he was cast in *Stella Dallas* in the same part played by Douglas Fairbanks, Jr., in the movie's earlier silent version. Holt appeared in numerous RKO Radio Pictures B films, but periodically he gained roles in quality productions such as *Stagecoach* (1939) and Orson Welles's *Magnificent Ambersons* (1942).

When World War II beckoned the young men of America to war, Tim Holt enlisted in the Army Air Corps in April 1942. He underwent preflight training at the Santa Ana Air Base in southern California and was later transferred a short way to the Victorville Air Base for bombardier training. He graduated from the school on 8 May 1943 as a second lieutenant. Holt remained at Victorville as an instructor until ordered to the Marine Air Corps training station at El Centro, California, where he helped the Marines establish a high-altitude bombardier training school. He then went to the Bureau of Naval Aeronautics in Washington, D.C., to work with the Marines and the Navy until 10 September 1944, when he returned to Victorville to prepare for overseas duty.

Before seeing action in the Pacific, Holt trained as a bombardier in B-29s at Lincoln Army Air Field in Nevada and at Alamogordo, New Mexico. He finally went overseas in April 1945 and flew his first mission against Japanese home island oil fields on 10 May.

Holt flew twenty-two missions in B-29 Superfortresses before the war ended. His last flight took place on the day the Japanese surrendered, and it was none too soon. Badly shot up, his plane crash-landed at its home base on Guam. Five and a half feet of the left wing had been shot away, and there were 175 bullet holes in the fuselage.

Famed cowboy star Tim Holt was a B-29 Superfortress bombardier who flew over twenty missions against the Japanese islands during World War II. On his last mission, the day the war ended, he was forced to bail out of his damaged aircraft as it approached its home base. For valor during combat he was awarded the Distinguished Service Cross and an Air Medal with three clusters. Shown here are B-29s departing from Guam on their strategic missions against industrial targets in Japan, May 1945. (U.S. Air Force)

Holt returned to the states in the fall of 1945 at the rank of captain; he was placed on the inactive list of the AAF on 10 January 1946. During his war tour Holt was awarded the Distinguished Service Cross, the Air Medal with three Oak Leaf Clusters, a Presidential Citation with one Oak Leaf Cluster, the American Campaign Medal, the Asiatic-Pacific Campaign Medal with three Bronze Star devices, and the World War II Victory Medal.

In 1938 Holt married Virginia Ashcraft, a student at UCLA at the time. They had a son, Lance, but the marriage ended in divorce in 1944. A few years later she sued Holt for nonpayment of support for herself and their son. A week after his first marriage was dissolved, the actor exchanged vows with Alice Harrison.

Following the war, Holt quickly revived his movie career. He appeared in films such as *My Darling Clementine* in 1946 and two years later in what was to become a classic film, *The Treasure of the Sierra Madre,* in which he costarred with Humphrey Bogart and Walter Huston. The film produced three Academy Awards: Walter Huston for best supporting actor, and his father, John Huston, for best director and best screenplay.

While continuing his career in films, Holt associated himself with a rodeo company. He bought into the Carl Lamarr–Joe Jennings Rodeo, which was headquartered in Norman, Oklahoma. In addition to becoming part owner of the show, he turned into one of its star performers. The company was known at the time as one of the outstanding rodeo shows in the country. Although he continued to act in pictures, Holt moved permanently to Oklahoma, settling on a small ranch near the city of Harrah. Of Hollywood, Holt declared, "I really never did like it."

Tim Holt died of cancer in 1973 at the age of fifty-four and was buried in an unmarked grave in Harrah. At the time he was general manager of country music station KEBC. In 1975 the Harrah Board of Trustees decided that it was time to recognize the respected actor. Oklahoma governor David Boren proclaimed 13 September 1975 Tim Holt Memorial Day. Kathleen Freeman, vice president of the Screen Actors Guild of Hollywood, dedicated Tim Holt Boulevard in Harrah. Letters came from, among others, Dennis Weaver, president of the Screen Actors Guild, and country singer Charlie Pride. In his letter, Weaver wrote, "The Screen Actors Guild, which represents all actors in the motion picture industry—some 30,000 in number—is delighted to compliment the city of Harrah for its recognition of our member Tim Holt. Tim Holt was a hero of his time: the embodiment of the best of Hollywood; and an individual beloved by his colleagues as a professional artist. His human characteristics are still remembered and cherished by all."

Audie Murphy

I n 1949 America's most decorated soldier, Audie Murphy, wrote a book regarding his World War II experiences titled *To Hell and Back*. It was a straightforward narrative of men at war. There was no reference by Murphy in the book to his awards, just a blood-and-guts story of what he and his men endured as they grimly fought a fierce German enemy in North Africa, Sicily, Italy, France, and Germany. Bravery and heroics were seamlessly woven into the story.

Audie Murphy was an extraordinary soldier. One of nine children, he was born on a sharecrop farm in Texas on 20 June 1924. When he was sixteen his mother died and the three youngest children of the brood were placed in an orphanage. The others scattered, looking for work. Audie found various odd jobs, among them pumping gas at a filling station and working in a radio repair shop. About that time the

(Courtesy of the Stan Smith Collection)

Japanese attacked Pearl Harbor and young Murphy was anxious to sign up and serve his country.

The famed Texan, small in stature but with a temper, was a fighter from early childhood. When he was in the fifth grade he attended school in overalls. Since he had only one pair, his mother washed them every night and soon they shrunk to the point where his schoolmates began to call him "short breeches." Every time someone joked about his appearance he ended up in a fight, something that eventually became an almost daily occurrence.

At the time of his induction into the Army at the age of eighteen, Murphy stood just five feet, four inches tall and weighed 112 pounds. He still displayed an explosive Irish temper, and when brought to the peak of rage he would take on all comers. The Germans were soon to face this fierce warrior, who before the conflict ended would spend four hundred days on the front lines, receive a battlefield commission, and win every American award for valor, including the coveted Medal of Honor.

Murphy initially tried to join the paratroopers and then the Marines, but was rejected by both because of his meager size. Upon the advice of an Army recruiter he loaded up on food, mainly milk and bananas, before taking a physical for the infantry. He passed and was sent to Camp Wolters, Texas, for basic training.

At Camp Wolters he showed signs of fatigue, and because of his youthful looks was nicknamed "Baby." His commanding officer tried to send him to cook and bakers school to keep him out of combat. Murphy rebelled and he was allowed to continue training as a rifleman.

As a youth Murphy often had to hunt for food for the family, and he became a crack marksman. That early experience worked to his advantage in basic; he soon distinguished himself by readily mastering all types of weapons. Later, in combat, he was quick in reacting to tactical situations, sizing up enemy intentions, and without hesitation attacking though often outnumbered. He had an almost uncanny knack of making quick, lifesaving decisions, and his inherent leadership qualities emerged as he was transformed into a disciplined, combat-experienced soldier.

Murphy's next duty station was Fort Meade, Maryland, where he underwent further training before going overseas. Shipped to North

Africa, he landed in Casablanca in February 1943 after being seasick during most of the convoy transit. He was disappointed to find that the American "Torch" campaign was nearly over. He learned, however, that as a private in Company B, 1st Battalion, 15th Infantry Regiment of the famed "Blue and White Devils" of the 3d Infantry Division, he was slated for action further east in Tunisia. Murphy was to remain with Company B during most of his combat service.

When Murphy arrived in Tunis, a mopping-up operation was under way and his unit was not needed. However, he was soon among the American soldiers who landed on the shores of Sicily on 10 July 1943. Still trying to keep Murphy out of the front lines, his commanding officer made him a runner. But after Murphy managed to slip off on patrols, his commander gave up, promoted him to corporal, and sent him forward. For the next two years Murphy remained in the thick of combat action. While in Sicily he contracted malaria, a malady that stayed with him for the rest of his life.

After a week's recuperation in a field hospital, he rejoined his unit, now part of the Sixth Army under Lt. Gen. George Patton. Murphy found himself in a forced march over rough terrain toward the city of Palermo, which was situated on the northwestern tip of the island. The march became almost a foot race, for the troops managed to cover from twenty-five to thirty miles a day. His and the other American units did not know that Patton and General Montgomery (who commanded the British Eighth Army, which was sweeping up the eastern shore of the island) were in a race to reach Messina first. Skirmishes with well-fortified German defenders along the northern coast gave Murphy his first taste of combat. His unit was caught in a concentration of artillery and mortar fire as it neared Mount Furiano just west of Messina, leaving dead and wounded American soldiers littered along the approaches to the mountain. This was the first time Murphy heard the screams of the wounded and witnessed the disciplined and ruthless enemy he faced. He quickly realized what fury lay ahead. A coordinated attack with a surprise landing from the rear neutralized the enemy defenses and the mountain was bypassed; the Americans reached Messina two hours before the first British elements arrived. With the fall of Sicily, the Allies debated their next move. If they crossed the Straits of Messina and fought their way up the Italian boot, they could force the Italians out of the war and tie down German troops that might otherwise go to France and Russia as reinforcements. The other option was to concentrate on the coming invasion of France, which would demand all of their resources. When the Italian government fell on 25 July 1943, the decision was made to move against the mainland of Italy.

On 3 September General Montgomery crossed the straits with the British Eighth Army and moved northward to join up with U.S. general Mark Clark, who landed his Fifth Army on the beaches just south of Salerno, fifty miles from Naples. Clark's forces consisted of the British X Corps and the U.S. VI Corps. Among the various units assigned to the VI Corps was the 3d Infantry Division. By the time the 3d came ashore, it was apparent from the American and British dead and wounded littering the beach that the Allies had paid dearly for the assault.

Driving northward toward Naples, Murphy's unit soon ran into stiff enemy resistance. It was at this time that Murphy's fierce fighting earned him a promotion to sergeant and leadership of his own squad. In one instance he and his men encountered a German patrol at dusk and had to shoot their way out of an ambush. Hiding until morning in a rock quarry, Murphy's men killed and captured seven Germans who had been sent to eliminate his unit. Murphy often showed compassion for enemy soldiers who no longer posed a threat to his unit. It was typical for him to place his own coat over a dying German soldier to shield him from the rain. He also could not bring himself to kill fifteen-year-old German boys who were thrown into battle by Hitler. As he stated in later interviews, "I was young enough, but these were children. I couldn't shoot them."

The 3d Infantry Division soon went into training for the invasion of Anzio south of Rome. The sea-launched assault was designed to intercept the German supply lines that supported the intense fighting to the south at Monte Cassino, where the British Eighth and the American Fifth Armies were being held at bay.

Eisenhower didn't favor the Anzio plan because he did not think he had the forces to hold a new beachhead and also fight his way east to the Alban Hills to breach the German supply lines. He soon left the battle area for England, where he would concentrate on the forthcoming Normandy invasion.

Churchill, however, continued to insist that an Anzio operation would successfully break the deadlock to the south, and on 22 January 1944, two divisions of the U.S. VI Corps landed on beaches north of the Gustav line, a major defensive boundary the Germans had established across the Italian peninsula south of Rome. Murphy had been hospitalized during the training for the invasion with another serious bout of malaria. Nevertheless, he rejoined Company B on 27 January 1944 and found himself in the middle of a furious engagement to hold onto the beachhead.

Though the Anzio invasion came as a surprise to the Germans, Field Marshal Albert Kesselring, commander in chief of German forces in Italy, quickly reacted to stop the Allied troops who were preparing to move inland. His local garrison force held on until reinforcements arrived from France, Yugoslavia, Germany, and northern Italy. Within two days there were forty thousand German troops in the beachhead area supported by tanks and artillery. Hemmed in all around, the Allied force was ordered to dig in and hold the beachhead. Murphy later remembered that it was the only time during the war that he felt doomed.

Murphy remained at the front, volunteering for reconnaissance patrols and fighting off probing attacks by the Germans. He was felled again with malaria and was taken to a hospital, but within ten days he was back with his unit. Before the breakout from Anzio he was offered a field commission as a second lieutenant. He turned the offer down since it would mean that he would be transferred to another outfit. (At that time the Army theorized that enlisted men would not respect an officer who had been commissioned from their ranks.)

The Germans were denied a push to the sea by heavy rains, which turned the land into bogs that could not support armor. With the coming of spring the ground began to dry, and Murphy's unit was positioned near a road that led to the enemy lines. He reasoned that German armor would use the road to spearhead a drive that could force the Allied troops to abandon the beachhead. He and his men mined the road and waited. Within a few days German tanks rumbled toward them, and the lead tank was blasted by a mine explosion. The Germans retreated but did not give up their plan to use the road. On the night of 2 March 1944, Murphy volunteered to lead a seven-man patrol to destroy the disabled tank. As they approached the tank, they could hear German voices and sighted several soldiers attempting to repair the vehicle. Leaving his men behind, Murphy crept near the tank and hurled two Molotov cocktails at it, but they failed to ignite. He quickly followed with a hand grenade, which landed inside the tank through the open hatch. The explosion didn't appear to do much damage, but it sent the German repair troops scurrying back to their lines. German infantry, guarding the tank from surrounding dug-in positions, began to fire at the lone intruder. Murphy set up a rocket launcher and blew the treads off one side of the tank, then made a quick retreat back to his men with bullets flying around him. The Germans abandoned the crippled tank and Murphy received his first medal, a Bronze Star with "V" device, for his daring feat. The V device signified that his medal was won in combat. The following May he was to win a second Bronze Star for exemplary conduct in ground combat against the enemy.

Finally, on 23 May, the 3d Division attacked the German ring around Anzio in force. The encirclement was breached but at a heavy cost. The division suffered 995 battle casualties. Murphy was in the front line of attack. By then he was well known in the division for his refusal to retreat. His strategy throughout the war was one of audacity, an approach that he discovered early in combat often confused the enemy and threw them off balance. To Murphy it was not courage or foolishness, but a tactical weapon.

The reinforced division fought its way to Rome and then went into amphibious training for Operation Anvil. The landing in southern France took place on 15 August 1944. As part of the Seventh Army, the 3d Infantry Division went ashore between Cavalaire-sur-Mer and St. Tropez.

Murphy landed on Yellow Beach, and although some historians regard the German resistance there as light, Murphy recalled that their casualties were heavy. It took them some forty minutes to capture a single coastal gun. Within four hours after the landing, the 3d Infantry Division had reached the high ground three miles from the beach. They spotted a cannon projecting from a rocky emplacement. Murphy's battalion was ordered to take the gun, which meant an uphill climb. The terrain was covered with scrub oak and brush, perfect for hiding German snipers. The men moved up the hill. All was quiet until Murphy heard the roar of enemy machine-gun fire ahead, followed by silence.

The men of Company B had been caught in an ambush, and many lay wounded and dead. Murphy, carrying a carbine and grenades, sized up the situation quickly. He knew that Company A was moving up on the right flank and soon would hit the Germans hidden behind a thick canebrake. What remained of Company B were pinned down by the enemy. If they moved forward or to the rear they would be exposed to intense enemy fire. As he moved forward, crawling toward the enemy, he spotted two German helmets just above ground in a chest-deep foxhole. Three other members of the machine-gun crew were sprawled flat, feeding ammunition belts to the gunners.

Needing more firepower, Murphy retreated back down the slope and borrowed a .30-caliber machine gun from a waiting platoon. Retracing his steps, he passed the point men of Company B. Reaching a position of advantage, he raked the German nest with fire and wounded two of the enemy soldiers. As he fired he noticed an infantry man next to him supporting him in his attack. It was Pvt. Lattie Tipton, his closest friend. They had fought together since Sicily. Tipton often talked about his daughter, Claudean, back in the states, and Murphy made a secret promise to himself that his friend would survive the war and see his daughter again. Tipton had part of his ear shot away, and Murphy yelled to him to fall back and get treatment. Lattie refused and advanced on the Germans beside Murphy. They finally made it to a ditch for cover, then crawled forward and came to within twenty yards of the machine gunners. As they were maneuvering to get into position, German riflemen fired at them from surrounding foxholes.

Murphy and Tipton rushed the nest and killed the Germans, falling on top of them. When Tipton stood up to observe the battlefield, he saw that the enemy was waving a white flag. His last words before a German sniper shot him through the heart were, "They want to surrender, I'm going to get them."

At the sudden loss of his buddy, Murphy realized that the enemy knew his position. He grabbed the German machine gun, lobbed several grenades into the nearest foxhole and a few more to keep the enemy down, then stood up and with the German weapon at his waist killed the two enemy soldiers below him. Watching the American soldier's audacious action, five German soldiers in nearby foxholes raised their hands in surrender. Murphy quickly moved over the hill firing at everything that moved. When all was quiet, he waved Company B forward. As they closed in on their objective, they found the German gun to be a decoy. Murphy moved back down the hill and sat by his buddy, placing a pack under his head for a pillow. He took Tipton's personal effects, and at the retrieval of a picture of Claudean, he sat down and wept. For his heroic action Murphy was awarded the Distinguished Service Cross. He was cited for extraordinary heroism that resulted in the capture of a fiercely contested, enemy-held hill and the annihilation or capture of an entire enemy garrison. Later, Dave "Spec" McClure, a screenwriter who ghostwrote *To Hell and Back* with Murphy, believed that the loss of Murphy's friend changed him from an outstanding soldier to an extraordinary combat fighter who would thereafter continually lay his life on the line. During a postwar interview with McClure, however, Murphy disagreed. He stated that although the war became more personal for him after Lattie's death, it was the continuous and overwhelming combat experience that determined his actions. He saw the war as "an endless series of lethal problems, some big, some small, that involved the blood and guts of men. . . . The dead would lie where they had fallen; the living would move on and keep fighting. There was nothing else to do."

Soon thereafter Murphy led the first patrol into the French village of Ramatuelle, which had been abandoned by the Germans. Upon reconnoitering the countryside, he and two of his men spotted a German gun emplacement two miles southeast of the town. This time the gun was no dummy. Although he knew the emplacement would be manned by a force far outnumbering his small patrol, he attacked and surprised the unsuspecting Germans. After a brief firefight, they surrendered.

Once the beachhead had been secured, the 3d Infantry Division moved rapidly up the Rhone Valley. It soon reached the town of Montelimar, which was occupied by a large contingent of the 338th German Infantry Division along with segments of other divisions.

As part of the 1st Battalion of the 15th Infantry Regiment, Murphy and his men were directed to bypass Montelimar and close the only escape route, which was north of the town. Correctly guessing the American plan, the Germans hit the Americans with a full regiment. Though the American soldiers were dead tired from more than a week of continuous fighting, they met the enemy head-on in a fierce three-day battle before the Germans capitulated. The American battalion subsequently received a Presidential Citation for its "courage, gallantry and skill."

Up to this point, after a year of front-line engagements, Audie Murphy had not been wounded. That changed on 14–15 September during fighting near Vy-les-Lure. As Murphy returned from running an errand to the rear, he was caught in a mortar barrage. While he waited for the fire to clear, a shell exploded at his feet and knocked him unconscious. The stock on his rifle was broken in half, and one of his shoes was partially torn off his wounded foot. Fortunately, only a fragment of metal had pierced his foot, and he made it to the rear to have his wound dressed and get a new pair of shoes. Murphy was back in action in less than a week, having won his first Purple Heart.

By mid-September the 3d Infantry Division was bogged down as it reached German strongholds in the Vosges Mountains. The enemy had heavy artillery in place, dominating key highways the Americans needed to continue their advance. American artillery proved ineffective in routing the Germans. Frontal assaults finally forced the Germans to give way, but often only after hand-to-hand combat.

Nestled in the mountains was the town of St. Ames, which the Germans had made a linchpin of their line of defense. German artillery and infantry fire were positioned to stop any movement by the Americans down the Le Tholy-Gerardmer highway. The 3d Infantry Division had to break the German dominance of this road to continue its drive to the north.

The anchor point of the German defense line was the Cleurie Rock Quarry, which was situated on a hill with a dense forest. The quarry was a mass of tunnels and was protected from mortar fire by reinforced concrete walls. A vertical cliff stretching across the north side of the quarry provided further protection for the Germans.

The 15th Infantry Regiment was ordered to take the quarry by direct assault. On 28 September the 15th reached a position to launch an all-out attack. The next day the 1st Battalion approached the quarry but was stopped by furious enemy fire. Company B fought and held ground within fifty yards of the quarry. A ridge lay between the Americans and the quarry, and over the next four days the two sides exchanged control of the ridge numerous times. Murphy was later to comment, "We took and lost that ridge so often that some of the men thought we should be getting flying pay." It was during this ferocious battle that Murphy was awarded the Silver Star for saving the lives of an American reconnaissance patrol trapped by a hidden enemy machine-gun nest. Alone, Murphy made his way behind the rock-strewn cover of the enemy and surprised the Germans, who were about to finish off the Americans. He faced seven Germans, and within twenty seconds killed four of them and wounded the other three.

The Cleurie Rock Quarry cost the Americans too many lives and delayed the advance of the regiment. It was finally blasted to rubble by 105-millimeter assault guns, tanks firing at point-blank range, and a mortar barrage. Beyond the quarry lay another German line of manned foxholes at the bottom of a slope. The machine-gun nests were nearly impenetrable with rifle fire. On 5 October 1944, Murphy led the 3d Platoon of Company B down the hill to reconnoiter the situation. A German sniper dropped one of his men, and suddenly enemy fire swept the area, pinning his platoon to the ground. Six more were wounded before cover could be found. Murphy radioed the situation to head-quarters, and using a walkie-talkie radio, held his forward position calling in mortar fire on the enemy for almost an hour. The Germans had spotted Murphy and desperately tried to kill him, but as they inched closer he downed them with his carbine. When the fight was over, fifteen Germans lay dead and thirty-five more were wounded. For his heroics Murphy was awarded a second Silver Star.

Murphy was pulled from the front line and commissioned a second lieutenant. He took the promotion under the condition that he be allowed to stay with Company B. Long after the war was over one of the men from his company wrote him a letter stating, "You were never an officer to us. You may remember that it was your own 'doggies' who put you up for the Medal of Honor. I know that you personally saved many lives, including mine."

Soon after rejoining his company Murphy led his platoon through a forest where a German sniper killed his radioman, who was beside him, and a second bullet ricocheted off a tree and hit Murphy in the right hip, sending him sprawling to the ground. He was in plain view of the sniper, and the German tried to finish him off with a shot through his helmet. But Murphy was not in his helmet, and before the German could get off another round, Murphy swung around and fired with his carbine pistol-fashion, dropping the enemy soldier with a well-placed bullet through the German's head. Murphy was taken to the rear for medical treatment. Bad weather delayed his evacuation for three days, and gangrene began to ravage his wound. He subsequently spent three months in a hospital and had to learn how to walk again. Though limping badly, he voluntarily went back to the front, still sick from his injury, having been awarded his second Purple Heart.

When Murphy rejoined Company B, 1st Battalion, on 23 January 1945, the outfit was at full strength with 6 officers and about 130 men. The 3d Infantry Division had been ordered to destroy the Colmar Pocket, a German salient projecting across the Rhine into France between Strasbourg to the north and Belfort some seventy miles to the south. This was a formidable task as the enemy was well equipped with armor and men to repel any assault the Americans might bring to bear. In fact, they were strong enough to launch a full-scale attack against the right flank of the Seventh Army. In addition, weather conditions favored the Germans. The terrain was covered by knee-deep snow, and during the day temperatures remained in the teens. The frozen earth made it almost impossible for the Americans to dig in.

Beginning on 22 January, the 7th and 30th Infantry Regiments crossed the Fecht River and fought their way to the Ill River with the objective of capturing a large forest, the Bois de Riedwihr. The following day the 30th took the forest and approached two villages, Holtzwihr and Riedwihr. The unit had moved so fast that communications were not established with forward artillery observers and the infantry pushed ahead without cover. They were suddenly confronted by ten German tanks and tank destroyers and about one hundred infantrymen on the outskirts of Holtzwihr. The 3d Battalion was nearly destroyed. A few survivors made it back to the Ill River. The 1st Battalion suffered the same fate at Riedwihr. The 2d Battalion ran into a devastating enemy armor assault and was forced to retreat.

With the 30th Regiment suffering severe casualties and as a result becoming too disorganized to mount any kind of a counteroffense, the 15th Infantry Regiment was committed to battle on 24 January. After the 3d Battalion made the initial assault and was stopped by a German counterattack, the 1st Battalion, which included Murphy's company, leapt into action. Moving through the battered 3d Battalion, it reached the Bois de Riedwihr. With no artillery cover, the 1st was driven from the forest but refused to retreat further. The men fell into artillery shell holes and waited for a German counterattack. None came.

The night was freezing, and while Murphy was trying to catch some sleep, his hair froze to the ground. Still wearing bandages from his hip wound, he was knocked to the earth the following day by a mortar shell. Steel splinters, some of which he carried for the rest of his life, penetrated his lower legs. These wounds brought him his third Purple Heart. As the battle progressed, Company B lost men rapidly. Though wounded, Murphy was able to continue fighting during the remaining struggle for the Colmar Pocket. During the night the 1st Battalion fought its way back into the Bois de Riedwihr and set up headquarters in a farmhouse. Of the 134 men and 7 officers who participated in the drive, only 2 officers (one was Murphy) and 34 soldiers were still fit for combat. The others had been either killed or wounded or had succumbed to the freezing weather. After five replacements reached the battered company, the unit was ordered to the southern edge of the forest and directed to hold that position until relief arrived. They reached their objective on 26 January, and that evening the senior officer was wounded by enemy mortar fire. Murphy was now in command of the company he had joined as a private.

Murphy kept his men standing and stomping in the snow to prevent their feet from freezing. He formed his battle line using a tank destroyer and armored vehicles from the 3d Reconnaissance troop to cover his right flank. Company A, which was about in the same shape as Company B, was to his right. A second tank destroyer had been positioned some forty yards ahead of the lines. A forward artillery observer, Lt. Walter Weispfenning, took up a position between the two tank destroyers. Murphy set up a command post ten yards in front of the rear tank destroyer. In addition to a field map, a pair of binoculars, and a carbine, he had a telephone that connected him with 1st Battalion headquarters deep in the forest.

At approximately 2:00 P.M. on the twenty-seventh, the Germans commenced firing an artillery barrage at the American forces. This was followed by the emergence out of Holtzwihr of a German force of six Panther tanks and about 250 infantrymen wearing white capes to make them inconspicuous against the snow. Their objective was to take the forest from the Americans.

An 88-millimeter shell pierced the rear tank destroyer's armor and killed the commander and gunner. Following the explosion, which started a fire in the vehicle, the rest of the crew escaped the wreckage and ran for cover in the forest. The lead tank destroyer courageously fought the oncoming enemy until it slid into a drainage ditch when the crew tried to reposition it. Exposed to the fire of the German panthers, the crew abandoned the tank and raced into the forest. When Lieutenant Weispfenning's radio failed, he also retreated into the forest at Murphy's urging.

Certain that his men could not survive the German onslaught without American artillery counterfire, Murphy ordered his men to the security of the forest and stayed up front to guide and correct artillery fire. By now the Germans had neared his position, and without concern for his own safety he ordered artillery fire into the advancing German infantrymen. When asked how close the Germans were, Murphy replied, "If you'll just hold the phone, I'll let you talk to one of the bastards!" The response became one of the classic remarks of the war.

Having exhausted his carbine ammunition as he was about to be overwhelmed by the enemy, Murphy was going to fall back when he spotted the .50-caliber machine gun on the turret of the burning tank destroyer. "Then I saw Lieutenant Murphy do the bravest thing I had ever seen a man do in combat," said Walter Weispfenning in a written statement after the action. "With the Germans only a hundred yards away and still moving up on him, he climbed on top of the burning tank destroyer and began firing the .50 caliber machine gun at the krauts. He was completely exposed and silhouetted against the background of bare trees. Eighty-eight millimeter shells, machine-gun, machine-pistol, and rifle fire crashed all about him."

The tank destroyer commander's body was hanging halfway out of the tank's hatch. Murphy dragged the body out and threw it into the snow so that he could freely traverse the machine gun. Murphy later remembered, "I didn't know how I would get out of the situation, but for some reason I didn't care a damn." Murphy concentrated his fire on the infantrymen because he thought that the tanks would not continue their advance without their cover. An observer of the action, Sgt. Elmer Brawley, later commented, "The German infantrymen got within ten yards of the Lieutenant, who killed them in the draws, in the meadows, in the woods—wherever he saw them." Smoke continued to pour out of the burning tank, which offered Murphy some concealment. At one point twelve German soldiers, unable to see the point of origin of Murphy's fire, stopped in a drainage ditch right in front of him. They appeared to be frantically discussing something. Whirling his machine gun around, Murphy killed all of them. The Panthers began pouring shells into Murphy's tank, but to no avail. Weispfenning later remembered, "The Lieutenant was enveloped in clouds of smoke and spurts of flame. When the smoke cleared Murphy still held his position."

While Murphy continued his one-man battle, some of the Germans bypassed him and made their way through the forest to the farmhouse that served as headquarters for the 1st and 2d Battalions. Colonel Hallett, the regimental commander, quickly organized what men he had available, using typists and clerks among others, and repulsed the German attack.

The weather finally cleared and fighter-bombers from the 1st Tactical Air Force flew over the battle scene. Murphy directed artillery smoke shells over the Germans, who continued to advance. Although slowed by the strafing and bombing of the planes, they forged ahead, threatening to overrun Murphy. As a last attempt to halt the enemy, Murphy called down artillery fire on his own position. With this final barrage the Germans retreated toward Holtzwihr. By some miracle Murphy had not been hit by the murderous enemy fire, but his old hip wounds had opened and he was bleeding profusely.

With the Germans now moving back and out of range, he crawled off the tank destroyer and limped back into the forest. Moments later the tank destroyer exploded. For his gallantry in this incredible one-man, hour-long battle, he was awarded the Medal of Honor, the nation's highest military decoration. His citation for the award credits him with killing or wounding fifty German soldiers and confirms that "Lieutenant Murphy's indomitable courage and his refusal to give an inch of ground saved his company from possible encirclement and destruction, and enabled it to hold the woods which had been the enemy's objective." It further records that Murphy "made his way to his company, refused medical attention, and organized the company in a counterattack which forced the Germans to withdraw." Murphy later

The most decorated American soldier during World War II, Audie Murphy was awarded more than twenty-eight combat decorations, including the nation's highest military award, the Medal of Honor, and a field commission for valor against the enemy in the European theater of operations. He was killed in an airplane crash near Roanoke, Virginia, at the age of forty-six and is buried at Arlington National Cemetery. Here he is being congratulated for his Medal of Honor by Gen. John W. ("Iron Mike") O'Daniel, commander of the 3d Infantry Division. Murphy insisted that he receive the award in the field rather than coming to Washington for a presidential ceremony. (National Archives)

was not able to recall a strong counterattack. He stated that he led the men still alive in Company B back to their original position in the front line and there they held their ground until relieved the next day by the 3d Battalion of the 30th Infantry Regiment. That unit subsequently captured Holtzwihr. Murphy continued to lead Company B in spite of his wounds, until the enemy abandoned the Colmar Pocket on 6 February 1945. The 3d Division was awarded a Presidential Citation and a Croix de Guerre with Palm from the free French government.

On 18 February the 3d Division was ordered from the front for rest and reorganization before an assault on the Siegfried Line, which was to commence in mid-March. Fearing that their prospective Medal of Honor recipient would be killed before the award could be made, Murphy's superiors ordered him to assume liaison duties away from the front line. Murphy, however, took his new assignment a little too far. In fact, he ended up in a precarious liaison with the Germans. One day he and another officer, Capt. "Red" Coles, both riding in a jeep, ended up far into enemy territory. Rounding a bend they suddenly found themselves in the midst of four hundred enemy soldiers who were lying alongside the road taking a rest break. Murphy ordered the driver to continue on as if nothing unusual was happening. The jeep and its three occupants passed through the Germans acting as if they might be an advance contingent of a follow-on Allied force. They waved to the Germans, who waved back, and once past the line of soldiers, they hid until the Seventh Army caught up with them.

Murphy had pulled a similar bluff while he was engaged in the Colmar Pocket. During the final days he and his men had taken a group of German soldiers prisoner and had sat down alongside a road to rest. Suddenly they heard the unmistakable sound of tanks—German tanks— moving in their direction. Murphy immediately took off his helmet and put on a German helmet. His men followed suit. With their fatigues caked in mud it was hard to tell them from the enemy. As the tanks roared by, he waved to the Germans, and they, seeing German helmets, waved back thinking the group was a party of their own army.

When word came back that Captain Harris, who was with Company B, had been killed near the Siegfried Line and that the unit had bogged down, Murphy quietly gathered his gear, a carbine, and hand grenades, and conned a driver into taking him to the front.

Finding Company B, he took them through the Siegfried Line and instructed the lieutenant in charge to keep the men under cover until contacted by other units. By this time Company B, which had fought so valiantly, was suffering from battle fatigue. Later, after the war was over, Murphy received a lengthy letter from one of the men thanking him for his rescue of the company.

As liaison officer, Murphy had at his disposal a jeep mounted with a .50-caliber machine gun. He added grenades, several rifles, and two

German machine guns to his moving arsenal. He was determined not to be captured at this point in the war.

Murphy was invited to Washington to receive the Medal of Honor from President Harry Truman, but he declined the invitation, preferring instead to receive the award in the field. Gen. Alexander Parch made the award on 2 June 1945 in Salzburg, Austria. That day Murphy also received the Legion of Merit "for exceptional meritorious conduct in performance of battle duty," making him the most decorated American soldier of the war. His nearest competitor was Capt. Maurice Britt, also a member of the 3d Infantry Division. After the end of the war, Audie Murphy received the Legion of Honor Chevalier and the Croix de Guerre with Silver Star from France, and also the Croix de Guerre with Palm from Belgium. Murphy fought in six major battle campaigns: Sicily, Naples-Foggia, Rome-Arno, Southern France, the Rhineland, and Central Europe. For each of those campaigns he was allowed to wear a star on his theater ribbon. His most prized decoration, however, was the Combat Infantryman's Badge. During the war Murphy was credited with killing, capturing, or wounding 240 Germans.

Murphy was granted a furlough in June 1945, a month after the war in Europe had ended. He departed Paris by plane, and his first stop in America was San Antonio, where America's most decorated soldier was given a warm and enthusiastic reception. Next came his hometown of Farmersville, Texas, where another large welcoming affair was held and he met with his sisters, Connie and Billie. For the next thirty days he made numerous public appearances, after which he was invited to Hollywood by actor James Cagney to try his hand at movie acting. Murphy later said, "I'd rather return to the Colmar Pocket in France than face another 'welcome home' or review another parade. That's what I wrote my commanding officer, Colonel H. D. Eddson, shortly after I returned from France, and after 30 days of leave and with a 30-day extension ahead of me, it still goes. But you can't say no to people who are honoring you, and I appreciate all that has been done for me. It's just that I have so little time to myself."

Murphy was discharged from the Army on 21 September 1945. On that same day he went to Hollywood. Cagney, who met him at the airport in California, stated later, "I knew Murphy only from his photographs. In reality he was terribly thin. His color was bluish gray. I had reserved a hotel room for him. But he looked so sick that I was afraid to leave him alone. I took him home and gave him my bed." This was after a three-month rest from combat. The war had taken a horrible toll on his nerves. Years later he would tell an interviewer, "Despite everything, I loved the damned Army. . . . For a long time it was Father, Mother and Brother to me. It made me somebody, gave me self-respect."

In 1950 Murphy joined the 36th Division of the Texas National Guard, staying with the unit until he was promoted to major. The pressures of movie making finally forced him to place himself on the list of inactive reserves.

Now in glamorous Hollywood and supported by Cagney and other movie luminaries, America's most decorated and celebrated soldier of World War II soon found himself cast as the hero lead in low-budget westerns by Universal-International Studios. He made his film debut in *Beyond Glory* playing opposite Alan Ladd. Following several more films of that genre, MGM borrowed him to star in Stephen Crane's Civil War classic, *The Red Badge of Courage.* Murphy's best performance won him critical acclaim for the film. A few years later he played himself in *To Hell and Back,* based on his best-selling autobiography. For a short while he was cast in better quality pictures, but Murphy soon was back to playing westerns. He made his last film, *40 Guns to Apache Pass,* in 1966. During his motion picture career he appeared in more than forty films.

Murphy married actress Wanda Hendrix in 1949, but they were divorced a few months later. In 1951 he married Pamela Archer, an airline stewardess, with whom he had two children, Terry and James. Murphy became a successful racehorse owner and breeder, having interests in such renowned horses as Depth Charge.

Money meant little to Murphy, and in time he became a compulsive gambler, losing much of the fortune he made from his book and his films. Like many veterans of World War II, he suffered from posttraumatic stress disorder (PTSD) and was plagued by insomnia. At the time, PTSD was not recognized and no treatment was available. Those afflicted with PTSD often became alcoholics, ended up in mental wards, or committed suicide. It has been written that for many years Murphy slept with a loaded gun under his pillow.

Audie Murphy was killed at the age of forty-six while on a business trip. On 28 May 1971 a privately owned Aero Commander aircraft he was on crashed into rugged Brushy Mountain near Roanoke, Virginia. America's most decorated soldier of World War II was buried with full military honors at Arlington National Cemetery on 7 June of that year.

In 1996 the Texas Legislature officially designated his birthday, 20 June, Audie Murphy Day.

Murphy's grave is located in section 46 of Arlington Cemetery, near a monument commemorating the 3d Infantry Division. His simple white marker carries the words:

Audie L. Murphy

Texas

June 20, 1924

May 28, 1971

Medal of Honor

DSC

SS & OLC

LM

BSM & OLC

PH & 2 OLC

A listing of Major Audie Murphy's awards and decorations follows:

Major Audie Murphy:
Authorization for Awards and Decorations

Medal of Honor

Distinguished Service Cross

Silver Star with First Oak Leaf Cluster

Legion of Merit

Bronze Star Medal with "V" Device and First Oak Leaf Cluster

Purple Heart with Second Oak Leaf Cluster

Good Conduct Medal

Distinguished Unit Emblem with First Oak Leaf Cluster

American Campaign Medal

European–African–Middle Eastern Area Campaign Medal with One
   Silver Star, Four Bronze Service Stars (representing nine Campaigns)

and one Bronze Arrowhead (representing assault landing at Sicily
and Southern France)
World War II Victory Medal
Army of Occupation Medal with Germany Clasp
Armed Forces Reserve Medal
Combat Infantryman Badge
Marksman Badge with Rifle Bar
Expert Badge with Bayonet Bar
French Fourragere in Colors of the Croix de Guerre
French Legion of Honor, Grade of Chevalier
French Croix de Guerre with Silver Star
French Croix de Guerre with Palm
Medal of Liberated France
Belgian Croix de Guerre 1940 Palm

Bert Parks

P ast winners of the Miss America Pageant are often forgotten, but not former master of ceremonies Bert Parks. Appreciative audiences for years eagerly anticipated Parks's rendition of "There She Is, Miss America" as the tearful Miss America paraded down the runway at Atlantic City. Parks was the host of numerous radio and television shows and appeared in two movies, *That's the Way of the World* (1975) and *The Freshman* (1990). He was a noted entertainer who served his country with honor during World War II.

Bert Parks was born in Atlanta, Georgia, on 30 December 1914 to Aaron Jacobson, a merchant, and Hattie (Spiegel) Jacobson. He attended Marist College, a boy's Catholic preparatory school, and he got his first broadcast job at Atlanta radio station WGST as an announcer and errand boy. He eventually worked his way up to chief announcer.

(Photofest)

After two years at the station, Parks went to New York and auditioned for CBS radio, where he was hired as a staff announcer. At the age of eighteen he was the youngest network announcer in the business.

Versatile and enthusiastic, with a sparkling smile, Parks was soon doing much more than announcing. In time he was assigned to the popular *Eddie Cantor Show,* where he acted as straight man for Cantor and was also a vocalist. Parks served as master of ceremonies for the *Xavier Cugat Show* and was the announcer for the *Camel Caravan* program. Other well-known announcers at CBS at the time included Harry Von Zell, Paul Douglas, Ralph Edwards, Andre Baruch, and Mel Allen.

When America went to war, Bert Parks joined the Army as a private in 1942. Upon completion of basic training, he was sent to China, where he served as an infantryman assigned to reconnaissance operations, which included establishing underground radio stations behind Japanese lines. On one occasion he spent three weeks in enemy territory working with a wire recorder. Later, after he had received a commission and been promoted to second lieutenant, he was lost for ten days behind Japanese lines in Burma. Following such precarious duty he was assigned as an announcer for a weekly Army radio program from the China-Burma-India (CBI) theater.

Before his discharge in 1946, Parks was promoted to captain and served on the staff of Gen. Joseph W. Stilwell, U.S. commander of American and Chinese troops in the CBI. For his service during the war, Parks was awarded the Bronze Star Medal, the American Campaign Medal, the Asiatic-Pacific Campaign Medal, and the World War II Victory Medal.

Bert Parks returned to CBS after the war and became a popular host of game shows such as *Break the Bank* and *Stop the Music.* During the ensuing years the supercharged performer became one of the most popular master of ceremonies in radio and television, hosting a myriad of quiz shows, including *Party Line, Balance Your Budget, Bid 'n Buy, The Big Payoff, Circus, Double or Nothing, Giant Step, Hold That Note, Masquerade Party, Two in Love,* and *Yours for a Song.* During the 1950s Parks appeared on as many as twelve programs a week.

Parks likely was best known as the host of the Miss America Pageant from the mid-1950s until he was fired in 1980 because the show's producers wanted a younger talent. The dismissal caused a nationwide

Bert Parks spent most of World War II in the China-Burma-India theater, often operating behind enemy lines. Shown here is an American field artillery battery firing its 75-millimeter howitzer at Japanese emplacements along the Burma Road near the town of Namhkam. (National Archives)

sympathy campaign for Parks, but his tenure with the popular live pageant was over. In 1990 he made a special appearance at the event and received a standing ovation as he lip-synched his signature tune, "There She Is, Miss America."

During the 1960s and 1970s Parks made guest appearances on various television shows, such as *Ellery Queen, Burke's Law,* and *The Bionic Woman.* In 1961 he played Professor Harold Hill in the popular stage play *The Music Man,* replacing Eddie Albert. He appeared in 330 performances of the show and went on to appear in the Broadway musicals *Mr. President* and *Damn Yankees.* At curtain calls he would often sing the Miss America song.

Parks met Annette Liebman in 1942 while she was a student at Columbia University. They were married the following year before he was sent overseas. During their enduring marriage, the couple had twin sons, a daughter, and several grandchildren. Parks died in 1992 at the age of seventy-seven.

During his career Bert Parks appeared on every network and New York flagship station. He received the TV Forecast Award in 1950, the Poor Richard Award in 1957, the City of Hope Award in 1958, and the March of Dimes Man of the Year Award for 1963.

Sabu

Many actors of the 1930s and 1940s were "discovered" in modest circumstances, never dreaming they might someday be a major movie star. The beautiful Lana Turner was found sipping a soda at Schwab's Drugstore on Sunset Boulevard in Hollywood. Halfway around the world a twelve-year-old stable boy was noticed by a filmmaker and brought to England and then to America and screen fame. His name was Sabu Dastagir, or just Sabu.

Sabu Dastagir was born in Karapur, Mysore City, India, on 27 January 1924. His father, Shaik Ibraham, died when Sabu was a small child. Ibraham was a mahout in the service of the Maharajah of Mysore. Sabu's uncle, Shaik Hussaim, was in charge of the Maharajah's two hundred elephants, and Sabu helped care for the animals.

Robert Flaherty was making a film for producer Alexander Korda in Mysore in 1936 when he took notice of the young boy and his uncanny skill with elephants. Sabu was a handsome child with a dazzling smile and an infectious personality. Flaherty brought Sabu to London, where he studied acting and several years later was cast in the British films *Elephant Boy* (1937), *Drums* (1938), and *The Thief of Bagdad* (1940). Shortly thereafter Sabu moved on to Hollywood, where he appeared in similar movies, frequently playing in exotic adventures opposite Jon Hall and Maria Montez. Their first together was *Arabian Nights* in 1942.

Sabu gained U.S. citizenship, and in September 1943 he enlisted in the U.S. Army Air Forces. After completing basic training, he was sent to gunnery school at March Field, California. Within a short time Sabu found himself in the South Pacific attached to the 424th Bomb Squadron, 307th Bomb Group (known as "the Long Rangers" for their extended missions) of the Thirteenth Air Force, flying in B-24 Liberator bombers as a ball turret gunner. Despite his movie celebrity, he expected no favors, and he was liked by everyone in the squadron. Sabu's station in the aircraft was in an electrically operated retractable turret that housed two .50-caliber M-2 machine guns. It was positioned on the underside of the fuselage aft of the bomb bay.

The Thirteenth Air Force operated in the China defensive; at Guadalcanal, the Solomon Islands, and New Guinea; in the Eastern Mandates and the Bismarck Archipelago; at Leyte Gulf and Luzon in the Philippines; and in the later China offensive. It remained in the Philippines, as part of the Far East Air Forces, after the war. Its first commander, Maj. Gen. Nathan F. Twining, became one of the noted "bomber generals" who directed the U.S. Air Force as an independent service in the years following the end of the war.

By the time his war tour was over, Sabu had merited the Distinguished Flying Cross, the Air Medal with four Oak Leaf Clusters, the American Campaign Medal, the Asiatic-Pacific Campaign Medal with four Bronze Star devices, and the World War II Victory Medal. He had flown more than forty combat missions in the South Pacific and had seen action from New Guinea to the Philippines. When Sabu was discharged in 1945, he had served for two and a half years in the AAF.

Sabu Dastagir, "the Elephant Boy," was an established film star when America entered World War II. His nickname originated when he was discovered by a British filmmaker in India, where he was a keeper of the Maharajah's herd of elephants. Sabu eventually performed in exotic movies that featured kings, palaces, harems, and elephants. He enlisted in the AAF on 4 January 1944, the same day he became a U.S. citizen. Trained as a retractable-nose turret gunner in B-24 Liberators, he saw combat in the Pacific theater and completed forty-two missions while attached to the 307th Bomb Group (HV), the Long Rangers. He was awarded the Distinguished Flying Cross and the Air Medal with four clusters. (Courtesy of the Academy of Motion Picture Arts and Sciences)

Upon Sabu's return to civilian life and his screen career, the demand for *Arabian Nights*–type stories had waned. After delivering a fine performance in *Black Narcissus* (1946), he was cast in a succession of low-grade films. His last movie, *A Tiger Walks*, was released in 1964. He and his wife, actress Marilyn Cooper, had two children, Paul and Jasmine.

Beset by personal problems in addition to his flagging screen career, Sabu died of a heart attack in 1963 at the age of thirty-nine.

Jimmy Stewart

Jimmy Stewart was one of the greatest American movie stars of all time. Stewart played everyman as the leading man, and his movies have become timeless images of the American way of life. He never strayed from the values he learned as a young man brought up in Indiana, Pennsylvania. His father and mother instilled in him the ideals of family, faith, and friendship—constants that remained with him throughout his life. Actor Charlton Heston once said of Stewart, "He was the quintessence of the American; if we are not Jimmy Stewart, we would like to be."

When Jimmy Stewart's father went to war in 1917, a Stewart had fought in every American war since the Revolution. Born in 1908, Jimmy missed his father but took pride in his parent's self-sacrifice, patriotism, and valor. Following a family tradition, young Stewart attended prep

(U.S. Air Force)

school at Mercersburg Academy in Pennsylvania. He then followed in his father's footsteps by enrolling at Princeton University in 1928, hoping to become an architect. An accomplished musician from an early age (piano and accordion), Stewart won membership in the Princeton Triangle Club and appeared in the club's annual musicals. It was at Princeton that he became interested in theater.

Stewart graduated from Princeton in 1932. Because the country was in the throes of the Great Depression, however, there was little in the way of employment that he could look forward to. Stewart's best option, to join his family's hardware business, dissolved when the store burned to the ground that year.

Later in the year, one of Stewart's classmates, future director and playwright Joshua Logan, persuaded him to join the University Players in Falmouth, Massachusetts. Among those he met were Henry Fonda and Margaret Sullivan, both of whom became lifelong friends. Many saw a unique quality in Stewart, different from any other aspiring actor. His often awkward, shy manner, and down to earth personality, appealed to all he worked with. When around him, others felt an almost magnetic presence. One of his later costars, June Allyson, commented that "one could never tell the difference between his acting and real self. They were one and the same."

Sullivan took Stewart under her wing and taught him the art of acting. She spent long hours with him going over scripts and teaching him stage presence. When one of the group's little theater plays, *Carrie Nation,* achieved some success, the cast was bundled off to New York and booked into a Broadway theater. But prohibition was about to be repealed, and with ticket sales falling off because of growing entertainment opportunities, the show closed in three weeks. The cast journeyed back to their theater on Cape Cod, but Stewart and Fonda decided to stay on in New York and try their luck on the stage.

The two managed to survive on small roles, but whereas Fonda had to struggle for every part, the work seemed to fall into Stewart's lap. It was that way when he went to Hollywood as well. A talent scout saw Stewart and asked him to come to California for a screen test. He went and he passed it with ease. Stewart was young, tall, and handsome, and some in the business saw possible stardom in him. Henry Fonda began his career at Twentieth Century Fox, and the two soon became known as young studs around Hollywood, taking out a different starlet every night. When queried about the ladies, Jimmy would only say that they were great dancers and he loved to dance.

Stewart appeared in numerous MGM movies in the thirties, but it was *Mr. Smith Goes to Washington* (1939) that produced his first Academy Award nomination. A year later Katherine Hepburn insisted that Stewart appear in her new film, *The Philadelphia Story;* his performance won him an Oscar as best actor. He had expected his friend Henry Fonda to reap the award for his brilliant performance in *The Grapes of Wrath.*

Stewart owned a Stinson 105 airplane and spent many of his leisure hours aloft. But his attention was not diverted from the growing turmoil in Europe. Many Americans, including Stewart, were anxiously watching Hitler's blitzkrieg on the Continent and preparing for America's seemingly certain entry into the war.

Stewart was drafted in 1940 but could not pass the Army physical because at 150 pounds he was underweight for his six-foot, three-inch height. He promptly went about adding pounds by lifting weights and eating tuna fish sandwiches (his favorite)—lots of them. He gave the physical another try and this time passed it; he was inducted into the Army Air Force in March 1941. After completing basic training at Fort MacArthur in Los Angeles, he was ordered to report for duty at Moffett Field, California. Though a naval air station today, Moffett at that time was serving as an AAF base. Jimmy wanted to fly, and with two hundred hours of civilian time and a commercial license, he pressed for Army flight training. In order to increase his hours, he gave up his weekend passes to take flying lessons, paying for them out of his own pocket. Though he accumulated an additional one hundred hours, the military was not impressed and deemed that the famed movie star would have to work harder if he was to realize a flying commission. Stewart eventually went before a proficiency board and was required to take a flight test, which he passed. He was commissioned in January 1942. By that time, America was at war.

Though Stewart applied for overseas combat duty, he was turned down and sent to flight instructor school at Kirtland Field, New Mexico, where he learned to fly four-engine bombers. Soon thereafter he was promoted to first lieutenant and instructed pilots in AT-6, AT-9, and

B-17 aircraft. He also flew bombardiers in training. He was transferred next to Hobbs Field, New Mexico, for training in heavy bombers. Stewart was checked out as an aircraft commander and anticipated finally going overseas and into combat, but that was not to be. Instead he was sent to Second Air Force Headquarters at Salt Lake City and assigned as "static personnel," which meant he was to serve as an instructor pilot in B-17s.

Before long, however, an incident occurred during one of Stewart's instructor flights that brought his skill and experience to the attention of his superiors. During a night flight, a green navigator took Stewart's seat in the aircraft while Stewart was checking out other equipment. Suddenly, one of the engines exploded, sending metal fragments crashing into the fuselage, knocking out the trainee pilot in the right seat. In shock, the young navigator froze at the controls instead of hitting the fire extinguisher switch. Stewart rushed to the cockpit and pulled the navigator from his seat. He then hit the switch, and the engine fire gradually extinguished itself. Stewart brought the plane home and landed on three engines.

At the time the 445th Bomb Group at Sioux City, Iowa, was in need of an operations officer and Stewart got the job. He was particularly pleased because he knew that the group was soon to deploy to England. Within a short time he was made commanding officer of one of the group squadrons, the 703d. The 445th was stationed in Tibenham, Norfolk, England. It included four squadrons: the 700th, 701st, 702d, and Stewart's 703d. The bomb group flew B-24H, J, L, and M model Liberators.

Jimmy Stewart's first taste of combat, a raid on the naval base at Kiel, Germany, came shortly after he arrived in England. On the 7 January 1944 mission, his group came under heavy attack by Luftwaffe fighters over Belgium. As he approached the target with bomb doors open, an antiaircraft shell burst under the port wing, causing the plane to reel to starboard. Stewart managed to set the aircraft back on course, but as they were heading home the navigator radioed to Stewart that the lead formation, the 389th from Hethel, was off course and heading west over the dangerous skies of northern France and German intercept bases.

Stewart made the decision to divert his group, joining the straying 389th Liberators, which would need his firepower. He pulled his tight formation in behind the 389th aircraft, and the bombers soon were tangling with enemy fighters. During the melee the 389th lost eight aircraft. All of Stewart's 445th bombers survived the air battle. He was credited with preventing the destruction of the 389th by his daring action.

By the time his combat tour was over, Stewart had flown twenty combat missions. He was awarded the Distinguished Flying Cross for a raid on the German aircraft factory at Braunschweig, an Air Medal for a raid on Bremen, and an Oak Leaf Cluster for bombing Berlin. Stewart also was awarded the French Croix de Guerre.

It was notable that whenever Stewart led a 445th Bomb Group formation, no man or aircraft was lost. When he would consider the heavy casualties they often took during daylight missions and what might lie ahead for them the next day, he would reread the note that his father

Lt. Col. James Stewart is shown receiving the Distinguished Flying Cross Medal for a raid on the German aircraft factory at Braunschweig, Germany, during World War II. A B-17 Flying Fortress bomber pilot, Stewart flew twenty missions during the war. He was also awarded an Air Medal with one cluster and the Croix de Guerre. (U.S. Air Force)

had slipped into his uniform pocket before he left for the war, and along with it a copy of the Ninety-first Psalm: "I will say of the Lord, He is my refuge and my fortress. . . . His truth shall be thy shield and buckler." Stewart took comfort in those words and knew that they were all in God's hands.

On 31 March 1944 Stewart was promoted to major and transferred to the 453d Bomb Group as operations officer. In that capacity he was responsible for fifty bombers. By April 1945 he had made full colonel and was chief of staff of the 2d Combat Wing, Eighth Air Force. When released from the service in September, he had logged over eighteen thousand hours in the air. Stewart remained in the reserve until he retired on 31 May 1968 as an Air Force Reserve brigadier general. It was the highest rank in the military ever achieved by a movie actor.

After Stewart returned to Hollywood, the first movie he appeared in was Frank Capra's *It's a Wonderful Life* (1947). For his performance Stewart was nominated for an Academy Award; over the years the film has become a holiday classic. In August 1949 he married Gloria Hatrick McLean, a beautiful former model who appeared to be a perfect match for the quiet, reserved forty-one-year-old actor. She brought two sons by a former marriage to the pairing, and later the Stewarts had twin girls. The Stewart family led a quiet, simple life far from the Hollywood social scene. One of their sons became a Marine officer and was lost in combat in Vietnam just three months after his parents had visited him during a USO tour in 1969. Asked about the loss, Jimmy responded that he was proud that his son had served and done his duty.

In the years that followed *It's a Wonderful Life,* Stewart appeared in numerous high-quality films, such as *Northside 777* (1948), Alfred Hitchcock's *The Rope* (1948), *The Stratton Story* (1949), *Harvey* (1950), *Winchester 73* (1950), *The Glenn Miller Story* (1954), *Rear Window* (1954), *The Spirit of St. Louis* (1957), and *Anatomy of a Murder* (1959). In addition to *It's a Wonderful Life,* Stewart received Oscar nominations for *Harvey* and *Anatomy of a Murder.* During his long and illustrious movie career he appeared in seventy-eight films.

Jimmy Stewart remained a popular star well after he stopped appearing in movies. He enjoyed celebrity adulation for the remainder of his life. He was honored for life achievement by the American Film Institute in 1980, by the Kennedy Center in 1983, and by the Film Society of the Lincoln Center in 1990. In 1985 he received a special Academy Award "with respect and affection of his colleagues" for "50 years of meaningful performances, [and] for his high ideals, both on and off the screen." That same year President Reagan bestowed on Stewart the Medal of Freedom, America's highest civilian award.

Stewart lost the "love of his life" in 1994. A recluse after his wife's death, he enjoyed the company of his children and grandchildren until he passed away in his sleep on 2 July 1997 at the age of eighty-nine. It truly had been a wonderful life.

Jack Warden

J ack Warden has been one of the most enduring character actors
in show business. Born in Newark, New Jersey, on 18 September
1920, he was the son of Laura Costello and John F. Warden. His
father was a salesman, and young Warden attended school in Newark,
St. Louis, and Louisville, Kentucky, where he graduated from DuPont
High School. Warden served in the Navy, the Merchant Marine, and
the Army before becoming an actor.

By the time he was seventeen, Warden had won eleven of eighteen
bouts as a professional welterweight boxer under the name of Johnny
Costello (his mother's maiden name). He also played a season of semipro
baseball. But the country was in the midst of the Great Depression and
money was scarce, so at the age of eighteen he joined the Navy to get
three square meals a day and a paycheck of twenty-one dollars a month.

(Photofest)

Warden was ordered to a Yangtze River patrol gunboat in the East China Sea, where he served as a fireman first class. For three and a half years (1938–41) he watched as the Japanese marched on China. He recalls that the Japanese would yell at the patrolling American boat, "We get you, Yankee bastud, we shove the 6th Avenue El down your throats." He loved the duty, however, surrounded by high-spirited and hard-drinking young men. He often found himself in barroom brawls in Shanghai's Blood Alley, and with his ring experience he was usually the one left standing at the end of a pugnacious quarrel. When he was ashore, he occasionally played left field for the U.S. Asiatic Station baseball team.

Warden was discharged from the Navy shortly before the Japanese attacked Pearl Harbor. He got a job shoveling coal on East River tugs in New York, worked as a bouncer at Roseland dance hall in mid-Manhattan, and served as a lifeguard at the Park Hotel's pool. Eventually, knowing that a world war was in the immediate offing and still harboring a love for the sea, Warden joined the Merchant Marine and ended up working in the engine room.

As Warden later remembered, "My romance with the life of a sailor ended in 1942 while working as a water tender in the engine room of a freighter 30 feet below decks listening to repeated attacks by German bombers." In a convoy of ships headed for Alexandria, Egypt, the actor recalls being pounded for days on end by Axis aircraft. His method for surviving the ordeal and maintaining his sanity was to "just get through the next 20 minutes."

When his ship made it back to home port, Warden requested duty topside as a boatswain's mate. "When they refused," he later explained, "I went across the street and joined the army's 101st Airborne Division. I figured that anything was better than being trapped in the boiler room of a sinking ship."

Ten days before D day, 1944, Warden was a platoon sergeant and jumpmaster with the 501st Paratroop Infantry of the 101st Airborne. As jumpmaster, Warden had to jump either first or last. Warden's commanding officer decided to jump first, which left Warden to take the last jump. He bailed out at three hundred feet and seriously injured his leg when his chute failed to deploy from the low altitude. Warden was hospitalized for a year and left the service in 1946 with a permanent plate in his ankle.

Prime Minister Winston Churchill and Gen. Dwight D. Eisenhower observe one of the largest mass jumps ever attempted by U.S. Army parachutists. The demonstration was held by the 101st Airborne Division (which included jumpmaster Jack Warden's 501st Paratroop Infantry) at Newbury, England, 23 March 1944. (National Archives)

While Warden was hospitalized, a buddy interested him in reading plays. He had never even seen a play when he read his first one, Clifford Odets's *Waiting for Lefty*. It marked a turning point in his life. After eight months devouring as many plays as he could get his hands on, Warden decided to become an actor. Upon his release from the Army, he went to New York to stake out his future.

Because he had no acting experience, Warden's first couple of years in New York were disappointing. He took numerous odd jobs to keep himself afloat, but one in particular paid off far beyond the meager paycheck it offered. Warden signed on as a lifeguard at the old Park Central Hotel, where he happened to meet Margo Jones, head of a famed Dallas repertory company. She took a liking to him, and for the next five years he worked with her company, learning the art of stagecraft while being schooled in both classic and experimental plays. When Warden returned to New York, television was in full swing and he soon was appearing on *Playhouse 90, Alcoa Theater,* and other major television drama venues. His most vivid memory was of an appearance with Humphrey Bogart in a production of *Petrified Forest,* the veteran actor's only foray onto the television screen.

Warden made his film debut in *From Here to Eternity* (1953). Several years later he gained acclaim for his role in *Twelve Angry Men* (1957). He has appeared in more than forty films and was nominated for an Oscar as best supporting actor for *Shampoo* (1975) and *Heaven Can Wait* (1978). The tireless actor has performed in numerous television movies, such as *Brian's Song* (1970), *Raid on Entebbe* (1977), *A Private Battle* (1980), and *Helen Keller: The Miracle Continues* (1984). His many TV series include *Mr. Peepers* (1952–55), *The Asphalt Jungle* (1960), *The Wackiest Ship in the Army* (1965), *N.Y.P.D.* (1967–69), *Jigsaw John* (1976), *The Bad News Bears* (1979–80), and *Crazy Like a Fox* (1984–86). Warden is still active in both films and television.

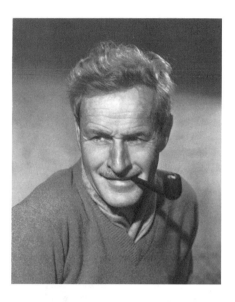

William A. Wellman

O ne of Hollywood's most prominent directors, William A. "Wild Bill" Wellman, appeared in one film, *The Knicker-bocker Buckeroo* (1919), starring Douglas Fairbanks. That was one too many for Wellman, and he decided that his career was behind the camera and not in front of it. Over the next four decades he directed some of the most notable American films of the twentieth century.

Born in 1896, Wellman attended school in Brookline, Massachusetts. With the advent of World War I he joined the Norton-Harjes Ambulance Corps, which was formed in New York for volunteer service in France in 1917. Two months after arriving in France he decided to abandon the ground war and take to the air in what was considered to be the most glamorous service of the conflict. He joined the French

Foreign Legion to avoid losing his U.S. citizenship and subsequently became a pursuit pilot in the Lafayette Flying Corps, a group of American pilot volunteers who flew for the French.

American volunteer pilots had been flying with French air squadrons under French commanders since the beginning of the war in 1914. They flew an assortment of fighter biplanes, primarily Neuports and SPADs. After the United States joined the fighting in Europe in 1917, the American pilots were transferred to the U.S. Army Air Service (USAAS) but remained under French command. American volunteer pilots who flew in the war were known for their reckless heroism and

Actor-director William A. Wellman served with the Lafayette Flying Corps, flying Neuport 11 and Spad S-VII fighters in France during World War I. He was shot down during combat and returned to the States. He was given credit for three confirmed kills and awarded the Croix de Guerre with two palms and five U.S. decorations. Wellman went on to direct many of the finest motion pictures made in Hollywood over the next five decades. He is seen here in front of his Neuport fighter in France. (National Archives)

determination in pressing attacks against such experienced German airmen as Max Immelmann and Oswald Boelcke. Wellman and squadron buddy Judd Hitchcock were among the most daring, often pursuing enemy planes deep behind German lines. If they could not down the aircraft they were chasing, they would strafe enemy positions and parked airplanes. In addition to William Wellman, other film figures served in French-led squadrons and the USAAS, including author and screenwriter James Norman Hall (*Mutiny on the Bounty*/1935) and director and producer Howard Hawkes (*Sergeant York*/1941, *Gentlemen Prefer Blondes*/1953).

Wellman was known as a fearless pilot and a crack shot, often flying alone at treetop level in an effort to harass the enemy as greatly as possible. He loved flying for the sport of it and was in the air constantly seeking out the enemy. He eventually was shot down by German ground fire and suffered severe injuries, for which he was sent back to the States. He would later say that he must have been the only pilot shot down by German antiaircraft gunners because "they couldn't hit anything." He was credited with three official victories. Following his recovery he was assigned as a first lieutenant in the USAAS at Rockwell field in California. For his wartime services he was awarded the Croix de Guerre (France) with two palms and five U.S. decorations.

After his discharge from the Army, Wellman became bored with several salesman's jobs and joined an air show, where he became a wing-walking stunt pilot. His film career supposedly got a start when he staged a landing of his plane on the polo field of Douglas Fairbanks's estate before a large crowd of celebrities and guests. Fairbanks immediately took to the plucky airman, and the legendary star subsequently gave Wellman his start at Goldwyn Studios. Within three years Wellman was an assistant director, and in 1923 he moved to Fox Studios, where he directed his first film, *The Man Who Was*. After several low-budget westerns, he directed the classic silent movie *Wings* (1927). Drawing on his World War I combat experience, Wellman produced a superb film, which won Hollywood's first Academy Award for best picture. *Wings* was the first of many Wellman films that dealt with airmen and their flying machines and brought to the screen a strong sense of documentary realism. Other air epics that followed included *The Conquerors* (1932), *Men with Wings* (1934), *This Man's Navy* (1945),

Gallant Journey (1946), *The High and the Mighty* (1954), and *Lafayette Escadrille* (1958).

Because of his maverick directing style, rebellious attitude toward studio executives, and feistiness on the movie set, Wellman was stuck with his old flying-days tag of "Wild Bill" throughout his film career. He was a heavy drinker, a tough talker, and a demanding taskmaster. He got into a fight with Spencer Tracy and nearly came to blows with John Wayne. His military experience was telling, and it influenced him throughout the rest of his career and life. He had seen an awful reality, and he was determined to tell the truth as he saw it in his films. As a result he often found himself at odds in Hollywood with people he believed were phony and values he saw as false. Many considered him irascible, but people who knew him best had great respect for the director.

Wellman's reputation grew in the 1930s as he broadened the scope of his filmmaking. During those years he directed such hit movies as *The Public Enemy* (1931), which established James Cagney in the industry; *A Star Is Born* (1937), for which he won an Oscar for best original story; and the French Foreign Legion movie classic, *Beau Geste* (1939), with its all-star cast of Gary Cooper, Ray Milland, Robert Preston, Brian Donlevy, and Susan Hayward.

The 1940s brought more success for Wellman, with films such as *The Ox-Bow Incident* (1943), which starred Henry Fonda, Anthony Quinn, and Dana Andrews, as well as two outstanding war movies, *The Story of G.I. Joe* (1945) and *Battleground* (1949). He continued to direct films until 1958.

Wellman was married five times. He finally found the right match with his last wife, Dorothy Coonan, who had acted in one of his films. He had seven children, and his son, William, Jr., appeared in a number of movies beginning in the 1950s. William Wellman died in 1975, and at his request his ashes were scattered from an airplane.

PART 2

Staff Personnel, Instructors, and Entertainers

Gene Autry

G ene Autry was an extraordinary man, one of legendary proportion in the entertainment world, yet few are aware of his
achievements during his sixty years in show business. He made
635 recordings and wrote or cowrote more than 300 songs. His recordings sold more than 100 million copies, and he was awarded more than
a dozen gold and platinum records, including the first ever certified gold
record. His platinum recordings include "Here Comes Santa Claus" and
"Peter Cottontail." Autry's version of "Rudolph the Red-Nosed Rein-
deer" has sold more than 30 million copies, making it the number two
best-selling Christmas single of all time (after "White Christmas").

Orvon Gene Autry was born on a ranch in Tioga, Texas, on 29 September 1907. Raised in Texas and Oklahoma, he went to work at the
age of seventeen for the St. Louis and San Francisco Railroad as a teleg-

rapher. He was working at a junction in Oklahoma when humorist Will Rogers happened to overhear him singing. Rogers suggested that Autry consider show business as a livelihood. Encouraged by the idea, Autry found work in 1928 at radio station KVOO in Tulsa. While still working with the railroad he collaborated with a train dispatcher, Jimmy Long, recording "That Silver-Haired Daddy of Mine." The recording eventually sold five million copies. According to a press release, the record holds the all-time sales mark for disks sold through the Sears, Roebuck mail-order house. Within a year Autry was known as "Oklahoma's Yodeling Cowboy."

Rapidly gaining in popularity, Autry signed a recording contract with Columbia Records in 1929 and the following year performed on the *National Barn Dance* radio program on station WLS in Chicago. Autry's first screen appearance was in the 1934 movie *In Old Santa Fe.* The following year he was given the lead in the serial film *Phantom Empire,* which led to a starring role in *Tumblin' Tumbleweeds.* Next came a string of westerns for Republic Studios in which he appeared with his comic sidekick, Smiley Burnette, and his horse, Champion. Autry's films were action-packed with little attention to romance. For a number of years the singing cowboy was the most celebrated of the western stars, and between 1938 and 1942 he was among the top moneymakers in Hollywood.

From 1940 to 1956 Autry starred on his own weekly CBS radio show, *Melody Ranch,* which featured his trademark song "Back in the Saddle Again." When World War II broke out Autry was determined to join the armed forces, and on 26 July 1942, during a broadcast of his program and at the Pentagon's request, he was inducted into the Army Air Forces as a technical sergeant.

Although Autry was in his mid-thirties, he had taken flying lessons and earned a private pilot's license, and his goal was to become a flight officer. He was sent to Santa Ana Air Force Base for basic training, then to Luke Field, Thunderbird Field, and Phoenix Airport for additional instruction before he was eventually accepted for flight training at Love Field in Dallas. On 21 June 1944 Autry won his service pilot wings and was promoted to flight officer. He was assigned to the 91st Ferrying Squadron of the 555th Army Air Base Unit, Air Transport Command, at Love Field.

While performing his flight duties, Autry flew many different types of aircraft, including AT-6s, 7s, and 11s; BT-13s and 15s; A-24s; C-47s, 49s, and 60s; B-25s; C-104s and 109s; UC-45s and 78s; and PT-17s. The C-109s were B-24 Liberators converted to tankers, which were often used to haul fuel in the China-Burma-India theater of operations. Pilots sometimes referred to the aircraft as C-109 Booms!

Autry made one trip to the CBI theater following a plan that took the flight by way of the Azores, North Africa, and the Middle East. The plane he was copiloting was en route to the Azores, a refueling stop for transatlantic flights, when it had to reverse course to avoid a typhoon and fly five hours back to Newfoundland, where it landed at Gander Bay with one engine out and low on fuel. Fog rolled in, and the crew was grounded for two weeks before proceeding to the Far East. After reaching Karachi, Pakistan, they flew to Assam, India, and then across the Himalayas ("the Hump"), which rise some twenty-nine thousand feet, to their final destination, Kunming, China. The supplies and ammunition brought there by ferry aircraft were most often destined for the 20th Bomber Command (B-29s) based at nearby Cheng Tu Airfield.

In his autobiography, *Back in the Saddle Again,* Autry reflected on the hazards of his flight to the Far East and noted that once was more than enough for him. During the remainder of his wartime service Autry did most of his flying stateside in C-47s.

When the air war ended in Europe, Autry transferred to Special Services and took a USO troupe to the South Pacific. Hopping from island to island, the group finally flew into Saipan on 1 August 1945. During their four-day stay, Autry noticed the frenzy of activity on the base; there were rumors that something big was going on at the island of Tinian a few miles away. He heard talk about a mysterious squadron training at Tinian and a bomb more powerful than anything yet seen in the war.

A longtime Texas friend of Autry's, Gen. Roger Ramey, was on Tinian with the Twentieth Air Force, whose operations were directed by Gen. Curtis LeMay. General Ramey invited the troupe over to Tinian for a visit, which Autry appreciated but thought rather unusual considering the rumors that were flying about. He surmised that the appearance of a USO group on the island would make things look more normal. Ramey entertained Autry days before the *Enola Gay* made its historic flight. He later recalled that the *Enola Gay* was only one plane

Flight Officer Gene Autry with an AAF pilot in front of a B-24 Liberator bomber. Autry flew the infamous "Hump" in the China-Burma-India theater while part of the Air Transport Command during World War II. (U.S. Air Force)

of a twenty-two-plane B-29 squadron. All the squadron's crews went through the same training exercises; no one knew until the last minute which aircraft would be selected to carry the bomb. Autry and his troupe were on Tinian when the first atomic bomb, code-named "Little Boy," was dropped on Hiroshima. After they returned to Saipan, a second bomb, "Fat Man," was dropped on Nagasaki.

When the Japanese surrender was announced on 14 August 1945, Autry and his troupe were on a plane headed back to California. Gene Autry was honorably discharged from the service in 1946, and the singing cowboy went back to work in Hollywood. During his war tour, he had been awarded the American Campaign Medal, the Asiatic-Pacific Campaign Medal, and the World War II Victory Medal.

In 1955 Autry received the following message from Headquarters, Continental Air Defense Command:

This Letter of Appreciation is presented to Gene Autry, former United States Air Force Technical Sergeant and Flight Officer, who served with the Air Transport Command, from March 1942 to October 1945. During this period, Flight Officer Autry performed duty as pilot on cargo type aircraft. Also during this period he volunteered his talents as a singer and entertainer for numerous Air Force shows. His weekly national radio show was continued with the name changed to Sergeant Gene Autry. His willing contribution to such worthy causes as war bond rallies, recruiting drives and entertainment of troops is a tribute to the fine character of this showman. Since his separation from the Air Force he has continually supported activities sponsored by or in behalf of the United States Air Force, such as . . . recruiting campaigns, support of Ground Observer Corps, and visits to Air Force Bases. The United States Air Force is proud to have Gene Autry as a former member of this organization.

> George F. Smith
> Major General, USAF
> Chief of Staff

While Gene Autry was off serving his country, Republic Studios had signed another popular cowboy, Roy Rogers, to replace him. Undaunted, Autry signed with Columbia Pictures. He later formed his own company, Gene Autry Productions. He continued his *Melody Ranch* radio series and in 1950 was the first major movie star to use the medium of television. For the next five years he produced and starred in ninety-one half-hour episodes of *The Gene Autry Show* for CBS television. He went on to produce other popular television series, including *Annie Oakley, The Range Rider, Buffalo Bill, Jr., The Adventures of Champion,* and the first thirty-nine episodes of *Death Valley Days.*

In 1988 a dream came true for Autry with the opening of the Autry Museum of Western Heritage in California. One of the finest museums of its kind, it is visited annually by thousands of children and adults eager to learn the fascinating history of the American West through a world-class collection of art and artifacts.

Gene Autry is the only entertainer to have five stars on Hollywood's Walk of Fame, one each for radio, recording, film, television, and live performance, including rodeo and theater appearances. Among the many honors and awards Gene Autry has received over the years are induction into the Country Music Hall of Fame, the American Academy of Achievement Award, and the Board of Directors Lifetime Achievement Award from the International Achievement in Arts Foundation. He also was inducted into the Nashville Songwriters Hall of Fame, the National Cowboy Hall of Fame, and the National Association of Broadcasters Hall of Fame. He received the Songwriters Guild Life Achievement Award as well.

An astute businessman, Autry held many interests in the community, including a radio and television chain, ranches, oil wells, a flying school, a music publishing company, and the California Angels baseball team.

Gene Autry, truly a legendary theatrical figure of the twentieth century, died on 2 October 1998 at the age of ninety-one.

Sammy Davis, Jr.

S ammy Davis, Jr., was a small man in stature but a big man when it came to theatrical talent. The son of vaudeville hoofers, he was on the stage at the age of four. Davis was a highly versatile performer who could not only sing but also dance, play an assortment of instruments, tell jokes, and do good impressions. By the time he was called into the Army, he had more experience and savvy than men twice his age. Unfortunately, the Army was a scorching experience for him.

Sammy Davis, Jr., joined the Army in 1942 and was ordered to Fort Francis E. Warren in Cheyenne, Wyoming, for infantry basic training. Up until that day, the U.S. Army had been segregated, a fact readily apparent to Davis and another African American enlistee who remained with him outside the barracks until all of the white trainees had selected their cots. Davis overheard the bitter words of those inside

(Photofest)

Sammy Davis, Jr., spent his Army service (1942–45) at Fort Francis E. Warren in Cheyenne, Wyoming. Already an experienced entertainer before entering the Army, he turned to his talent after he encountered racial prejudice during basic training and was denied overseas duty because of an athletic heart. He found that through his work on the stage, he was able to gain empowerment and respite from his tormentors. Here Fort Francis E. Warren troopers march through Denver, Colorado, during an Army day parade. (National Archives)

when the corporal informed the men that they had been assigned to the first integrated unit in the Army. To the obvious resentment of the barracks' occupants, Davis and the other black man were escorted inside and given two cots at the end of the room. They found that their beds were widely separated from the others.

A sergeant named Williams entered the barracks and announced that he was in charge of the company. He quickly noticed the unusual cot arrangement and ordered that they be moved into correct Army order. Sergeant Williams left the group with the admonition that no man was better than the next man unless he had the rank to prove it.

Davis was at first shocked and angry at the treatment he had been subjected to. He noticed others had begun to shine their boots. He decided to do the same to cool off and put the recent events out of his mind. As he worked on his boots, another pair landed next to him. They belonged to the man in the next bunk, who called him "boy" and said he could do his boots also. Davis bristled at the order and placed the boots back beside the man's cot. The man then proceeded to insult him with talk of a two-bit tip, but Davis would have none of it. He shot back that he was neither a boy nor a bootblack.

Unfortunately, the recruits turned on the other black enlistee, who accepted the subservient role assigned him by others in the barracks and found himself deluged with boots to be shined. Davis did not want to judge the man. Perhaps he had been accustomed to such treatment and humiliation. But Davis was determined to stay out of trouble and have a clean record.

Jennings, the man in the next cot, was suddenly on Davis's bed examining an expensive watch Davis had received from his uncle, Will Mastin, who headed the Will Mastin Trio, of which Sammy had been a member. Sammy asked for the watch back, but Jennings tossed it to another man across the barracks. As the watch was thrown from man to man as Davis ran unsuccessfully to retrieve it, Sergeant Williams suddenly appeared and assigned Jennings to a week of KP duty for his misbehavior.

Jennings threatened to retaliate. Many of the men in the barracks did not bother Davis, and once they began basic training they were too weary to care who the two black men were or what they represented. But there were about a dozen men, racists to the core, on whom Davis had to keep an eye. He avoided Jennings, their leader, whenever possible. One evening as Davis was putting on his watch, it slipped to the floor. Before he could pick it up, Jennings stepped over and crushed the watch with his heel, simultaneously remarking that he was sorry but Davis should not have left it on the floor. Davis picked up the pieces, too hurt to show anger at the time. He wrapped the watch in paper thinking that he might get it fixed.

Davis had been insulated by his vaudeville partners from the racial problems that permeated American society. His dealings with show-business people, white and black, had always been pleasant experiences, and although he stayed in hotels and rooming houses for "coloreds" only, he assumed it was because they were cheap. When he went into the Army he was still naïve about racial problems, and his first few days in camp were a revelation to him. The world now looked different. It no longer was one color. He had learned quickly and painfully about prejudice and hate. For Davis it was a shocking experience, a difficult awakening.

Sergeant Williams mentioned to Davis one evening as they walked out of the mess hall that he had reviewed his record and noticed that he had been in show business. He invited Davis to entertain at the service club, which held impromptu shows every Friday night.

After doing his first show Davis was cheered, and he went out front to have a coke. Some of the men from his barracks made room for him, and he was optimistic that he had finally won their respect. They offered their friendship, which he accepted eagerly. As he left to go back to the barracks, however, Jennings, who was sitting at a table with his buddies, stood up and asked Davis to have a beer with them. Coerced into joining the group, he was about to drink the beer when he got a whiff of what was in the bottle. One of them had filled it in the men's room. Davis placed the bottle back on the table and said to Jennings, "Drink it yourself, you dirty louse." With that, Jennings dumped the contents of the bottle over Davis; enraged, Davis sprang to his feet and took on Jennings, who was twice his size. Though shocked by the fury of the young soldier and gasping for air with Davis's hands around his throat, Jennings swung his attacker around until Davis released his grip and flew through the air, crashing into one of the tables.

The floor was suddenly cleared and Davis realized that he was in for the fight of his life. Jennings's first two punches broke Davis's nose, and a follow-on punch to the stomach sent him to the floor. Gasping for air, Davis went after Jennings again, though he delivered only one punch to every ten by his opponent. Davis fought on until he was beaten into unconsciousness, but he did get in his licks. After the fight was over, he learned that he had broken Jennings's nose, closed one of his eyes, and sent him to the infirmary. Helped back to the barracks by two of his friends, Davis was ordered by Sergeant Williams to join Jennings at the infirmary. But Davis would not give Jennings the satisfaction of seeing him there; he instead went to bed.

The needling from Davis's company, composed mainly of southerners and southwesterners, continued. Jennings and his buddies never let up. Davis got into scraps every few days. His nose got broken again, and in time the fights became a chore, but he always responded, often wondering why he had to prove something that no white man had to prove.

In his 1989 autobiography *Why Me?* Davis recalled another incident that compounded his anger. He was waiting in line at a wash basin
when the man in front of him finished and Davis stepped forward to
begin shaving. A hand from behind reached forward abruptly and
grabbed him by his t-shirt, pulling him back so hard that he hit the wall
at the opposite end of the room. The man who grabbed Davis said,
"Where I come from niggers stand in the back of the line." Davis got
up, gathered his toilet articles in his kit, and hit the man in the mouth
with the bag, knocking him down. Once again Davis stood over his
fallen antagonist ready to fight. The man made no attempt to get up
but lay on the floor and sneered, "But you're still a nigger." Sergeant
Williams witnessed the incident from the doorway and took Davis into
his office. Williams told him that the "nigger" thing would always be
there and that he had to fight with his brain instead of his hands. His
fisticuffs obviously were not earning him the respect he sought.

The company finished basic training and prepared for overseas duty.
Davis was rejected because of an athletic heart. Because of his lack of
education, most Army schools were closed to him, and since the Army
did not know what to do with him, he was sent back through basic
training—three more times. Once he got beyond his service-club entertainment appearances, he found that he was just another uneducated
laborer.

When Sergeant Williams encouraged Davis to read, the first book
he chose was *The Picture of Dorian Grey*. He bought a pocket dictionary to look up words he did not understand, and he often read on the
floor of the latrine, which was kept lit after taps. Williams started Davis
on an eager reading journey, first through Williams's own extensive
book collection and then on to a good portion of the post's library.
Having had little formal schooling, Davis was starved for knowledge.

One evening after a performance by Davis at the service club, he was
approached by George M. Cohan, Jr., who complimented him on his
talents. Cohan suggested that they pool their efforts and try out for the
intercamp entertainment competition. They subsequently auditioned
and were selected to appear in the show. Although Davis had recently
endured another humiliating experience at the hands of bigots, the success of that performance finally showed Davis that his talent was
indeed the weapon he had been looking for. It empowered him with an
identity that forced his white counterparts in the Army to back off; it

commanded their respect, which in turn, at least in his case, compelled them to suspend their prejudice.

At the end of the show Davis was transferred to Special Services, and for the next eight months he appeared in shows in camps around the country. He gave his all, and the audiences responded enthusiastically. When he finally was honorably discharged from the Army in 1945, he reflected on all that had happened to him and vowed never to suffer such treatment again. He would use his talent to propel himself to heights far beyond prejudice and hatred. He would work to become a star so that he could breathe like any other man.

Davis returned to the Will Mastin trio, which shortly afterward was billed as the "Will Mastin Trio starring Sammy Davis, Jr." They soon were playing in top nightclubs across the country. Sammy began to record on his own, and when television became popular, he took to the medium almost immediately. In 1954 his career nearly ended when a car accident cost him an eye. But the same determination and energy that had propelled him through earlier difficult times were not found wanting, and he was soon back in form.

Two years later Davis appeared on Broadway in *Mr. Wonderful,* and he made his movie debut in *The Benny Goodman Story.* He appeared in films with Frank Sinatra and was a member of Sinatra's "Rat Pack," a tight-knit clique of entertainers that also included Dean Martin, Peter Lawford, and Joey Bishop. Davis sustained his reputation as one of America's top entertainers despite criticism from blacks and whites concerning his marriage to Swedish-born actress May Britt, his adoption of Judaism, and his political metamorphosis from Democrat to Nixon Republican.

In 1989 Davis enjoyed critical acclaim as a costar in the movie *Tap,* the story of an over-the-hill song-and-dance man, and he subsequently went on a world tour with Frank Sinatra and Liza Minnelli. But the star had smoked nearly all of his life and, sadly, died of cancer the following year at the age of sixty-four.

Sammy Davis, Jr., had realized his ambition to become a major star in the theatrical world. In spite of the many travails he encountered, both inside and outside the Army, he honed his talent until few thought of him as black, only as a gifted performer who brought happiness to those who saw him on stage or listened to his melodious voice sing "The Candyman," "Mr. Wonderful," or "What Kind of Fool Am I?"

Melvyn Douglas

M elvyn Douglas, the suave film star of the 1930s and 1940s who romanced some of the most beautiful actresses of the time, including Greta Garbo, Claudette Colbert, Joan Crawford, Marlene Dietrich, Myrna Loy, and Irene Dunne, deserved then and deserves now to have his screen work more widely recognized. It wasn't until his later years, when cast as a supporting character actor, that awards came his way. He won the best supporting actor Oscar for his performance as Paul Newman's difficult father in *Hud* (1963). He was nominated for another Oscar playing opposite Gene Hackman in *I Never Sang for My Father* (1970). And Douglas won a second Academy Award in the supporting actor category for *Being There* (1979), in which he costarred with Peter Sellers. His work on television brought him an Emmy in 1968 for his performance in *Do Not Go Gentle into*

(Photofest)

That Good Night. This gifted director and actor of stage, screen, and television saw Army service in both World War I and World War II.

Melvyn Edouard Hesselberg was born in Georgia on 5 April 1901 to a Russian-born concert pianist and a housewife of Scottish descent. In 1918 he entered Army service at the age of seventeen. Hesselberg, like many others of that era, was anxious to go to France to fight "the Hun." But he never even saw Europe, let alone fire a weapon. His first Army assignment was as an aide in a hospital ward for venereal diseases at Fort D. A. Russell in Cheyenne, Wyoming. His observations of the ravages of these sexually transmitted diseases while at the hospital made him wonder whether he would ever get within an arm's length of a girl. Adding insult to injury, he was reassigned to a "venereal station" located just outside the camp limits. Any soldier who had been out on a pass had to be examined thoroughly before reporting back to his unit.

Douglas made sergeant, but the war soon was over and he was out of the Army. After being discharged, Douglas sought employment in Chicago. He tried various jobs, with little enthusiasm for any, including clerking in a men's furnishing store, working as a salesman for the Kimball Piano Company, and reading meters for the gas company. In 1919, however, having been drawn to acting in high school, he turned to the stage and made his acting debut. Douglas toured with various companies for the next several years and in 1928 landed on Broadway playing a gangster in *A Free Soul*. Several roles followed, one of which was in the hit *Tonight or Never*. The play was made into a movie in 1931, and Douglas went to Hollywood to reprise his stage role. Tall, dapper, and handsome with a debonair way, the thirty-year-old actor was made for the screen. He appeared in more than forty movies during the 1930s and early 1940s. World War II brought his career to a halt, however; in 1943 he enlisted in the Army.

Douglas was ordered to Camp Robinson, Arkansas, located just outside Little Rock. Two days earlier he had received a message from a friend in government that President Roosevelt was going to cut off enlistments over the weekend to anyone over thirty-eight years old. He was sworn into the Army in his pajamas the next morning and almost immediately bundled onto a southbound train with more than a hundred other recruits.

As a former movie star and one of the older recruits, he was initially given a hard time by his superiors; as time went by, however, they respected his earnest attitude, and he survived basic training. Douglas would often be called out of ranks to report to a colonel or major and instead find the officer's wife and other ladies waiting for him. He met and chatted with them graciously, accepting his role as a former movie star and the obligations that accompanied it. He finished training in March 1943, enjoying the best health he had experienced in years.

After basic training Douglas was sent to the Army Administration School in Washington, Pennsylvania, for instruction. From there he went to the classification and assignment section of an antiaircraft unit at Camp Wallace, Texas. In early April 1943 he was notified that he was under consideration by Special Services for "possible appointment" as a commissioned officer. Douglas completed all the necessary forms and waited. Nothing happened. What should have been a two-day process ran into weeks with no reply. Finally, an officer friend provided a possible clue. He told Douglas to reread his procurement document carefully. Douglas did, and he discovered the following clause: "The completed case should contain recommendations of the Commanding Officer of Candidate as to character, special ability of technical or professional nature." Douglas felt that he fit the job description. He read the paragraph again and the word "character" jumped out at him. Several congressional members had at one time interpreted his liberal politics as evidence of a character deficiency. He immediately suspected that J. Edgar Hoover's FBI had identified him, along with thousands of other liberals, as "controversial."

Douglas submitted a Request for Information form, which would force a response from the commanding officer of the camp. Within a few days he received notification that his situation was still "under consideration." Douglas suspected that he was caught in a political web and decided to seek a political solution.

On 14 May 1943 he wrote a letter to "Mrs. Eleanor Roosevelt," recounting recent events and relating his suspicion of a file that labeled him a "security risk":

I am sure you realize I am not merely concerned with obtaining a commission, as such. I want only to be as useful as possible, and if I can be of more use as an enlisted man than an officer, well and good; but it is of deep concern to me that there exists any "supposed evidence" which casts doubt upon my loyalty. . . . I would therefore indeed appreciate an opportunity to state my case. I am confident that an open-minded review of the facts would dispel any doubts and, more importantly, would allow me to function . . . solely according to what I am able to contribute. . . . I will be grateful for any help or advice you can give me.

Within a few weeks Douglas found himself in front of an Army board consisting of a colonel, a captain, some noncommissioned officers, and a clerk. He responded to their questions about his loyalty to America and was asked to recount his past political associations, which he did in detail. At the end of the proceedings the presiding officer ordered that the hearing transcript be sent to Washington.

Early in June, Douglas received a note from Mrs. Roosevelt, which included a copy of a memorandum she had received from the president. It read: "Very confidentially, I had this checked up with the War Department and they tell me that, while Military Intelligence did have some feeling about Melvyn Douglas being a Communist or associating with Communists, they have now decided to remove all this from their records."

A month later Douglas was commissioned a captain in the U.S. Army. He received orders for "permanent station outside the continental limits of the United States, temperate climate." He was baffled by the word "permanent." Soon he was shipped out from Camp Anza in Arlington, California. Upon arriving at his port of embarkation he discovered, much to his surprise and the surprise of others in his group, that they were to sail with a British crew who were taking over a new Lend Lease "Liberty" ship. As the American troops pulled up alongside the vessel, they noted that she was heavily loaded with all types of visible cargo and sat low in the water, meaning that her holds were filled as well. Early the next morning a pilot-officer came aboard to guide the ship from its moorings and navigate it through the harbor.

For the next fifty-nine days the ship plodded its way across the Pacific and Indian Oceans. Although Douglas and his men got on each other's nerves over that time, no enemy vessels were sighted and the crossing was made without incident. The ship docked in Bombay, and

Douglas found himself in the China-Burma-India theater, having been informed of his destination just two days before dropping anchor.

The situation in the CBI theater was highly complex in 1943. Chinese, Indian, British, and American troops were fighting to open a supply route through the Japanese-occupied jungles and mountains of northern Burma to link Calcutta, the head of the Indian railway system, with China. In addition to building a road (the Burma Road) through treacherous terrain, Allied forces had to contend with long-standing internal problems.

Gen. Chiang Kai-shek's Chinese army was made up of many troops loyal to feuding, corrupt warlords who were more interested in enhancing their fortunes than joining together to defeat the Japanese. In addition, the generalissimo expended valuable American aid to keep the Communist Chinese in check, even though they were staunchly anti-Axis. That tactic caused much tension between the American commanders and Chiang and his close advisors.

During World War II Melvyn Douglas served in the China-Burma-India theater by organizing entertainment for Allied fliers and soldiers. Shown are front-line troops waiting for the start of a show. (National Archives)

At the same time, the British were faced with multiple problems stemming from the desire by their colonial territories for independence from the Empire. Gandhi was jailed in late 1943 for insisting on non-cooperation with the British and nonresistance to the Japanese. Nevertheless, Gandhi's action led the British government to agree in principle to dominion status for India with the right of secession after the war. With this pact signed, the British were able to gain a volunteer force of more than two million Indian troops.

Douglas was assigned to a Special Services unit at Replacement Depot Number 2 in New Delhi. He emceed a 1943 Christmas program there that consisted of hymns in a recreational hall, a quartet offering favorite Christmas carols, a community sing, a transcribed Christmas broadcast from the States, and a bevy of entertainers.

Douglas put a series of shows together that at first did not seem to him a genuine part of fighting a war. He soon changed his mind, however, as he witnessed the soldiers of the "Galahad Force" (known as "Merrill's Marauders") standing in pouring rain and mud up to their ankles to watch whatever entertainment Douglas and his crew could offer. He often saw hardened soldiers cry when pop tunes from home were played. Within two months he was receiving letters from the GIs expressing their appreciation. Their thank-you's included such heart-felt expressions as "This little program was an oasis in the desert" and "Our starved feelings were greatly nourished." Douglas always treasured those letters.

Douglas's first troupe was formed in Karachi, and in a matter of time he had turned an hour-and-a-half's entertainment into a show. Comedians and singers were added, and it was not long before he laid out a tour and sent off a pilot group. He soon formed a plan for assembling such shows into what came to be called the Entertainment Production Unit (EPU).

Running the operation out of Calcutta with the support of a CBI headquarters colonel named Dean Rusk (later to be secretary of state in President Lyndon Johnson's administration), Douglas assembled a staff of seven to administer more than one hundred performers. His company soon produced three shows: *Magic and Music,* which gave 220 performances and drew an attendance of 89,730; *The Good Old Days,* which performed 129 times to a total audience of 121,350; and *Babe in Boyland,* seen by nearly 30,000 people at 59 presentations.

Because of his proven success in organizing and producing these all-important morale-boosting shows, Douglas was promoted to major. Celebrated stars began to find their way to the CBI theater. Lily Pons and her famed conductor husband, Andre Kostelanetz, Noel Coward, and others entertained at various CBI bases.

It was during that time that Douglas learned that his wife, Helen Gahagan Douglas, had been elected to Congress. Helen Douglas had been a Hollywood actress and an opera singer and was now a wife and mother. The Douglases had married in April 1931 after appearing together in the Broadway hit *Tonight or Never.* Douglas should not have been surprised at his wife's election to the House of Representatives. She had been a fighter all her life. During the Depression she organized a relief campaign for migrant workers; hers was one of the first brave voices to speak out against isolationism as the Nazis rose to power. She served three terms in the House before losing her Senate bid to a fellow congressman from California, Richard M. Nixon.

Following V-J Day, Douglas was ordered to Washington and New York to oversee the assignment of additional EPU personnel to prepare soldiers for leaving the Army. Efforts were made to get the servicemen to think about the world they would be returning to and their futures. Douglas remained in the New York Special Services offices until discharged in November 1945.

While still in the Army in New York, Douglas met two show-business veterans who were planning to produce a musical based on the wartime experiences of returning servicemen. As a producer of hundreds of CBI shows, he agreed to join their endeavor. The team's eventual review, *Call Me Mister,* was an all-veteran presentation with the exception of Broadway star Betty Garrett. The show was a smash hit, receiving high acclaim from New York's theater critics. Opening on 18 April 1946 at the Schubert-National Theater, *Call Me Mister* ran for seven hundred performances.

Once the show opened, Melvyn Douglas returned to Hollywood and was cast in a supporting role in the movie *Sea of Grass* (1947), starring Spencer Tracy and Katherine Hepburn. It was a shock to Douglas to find that after playing the lead in many movies before the war, he was now being cast in secondary roles. Though he appeared in several more movies, he found his film work increasingly unrewarding and in the early 1950s returned to the New York stage, where he achieved a reputation as a serious, highly respected actor. During his hiatus from Hollywood, he won a Tony Award for his portrayal of a presidential aspirant in *The Best Man*.

Douglas returned to Hollywood in the 1960s and appeared in some twenty additional films, his last being *Ghost Story* (1981). It was during that latter part of his career that he was awarded two Oscars as best supporting actor and an Emmy for his television work.

Douglas's wife of fifty years died in June 1980 at the age of seventy-nine. He followed her a year later at age eighty.

Clint Eastwood

I t is common for military aircraft to carry servicemen from all branches on a space-available basis. During the Korean War, two young Army privates found themselves at Naval Air Station Sand Point in Seattle, hoping to bum a ride back to an airfield close to their home base in Oakland after visiting some lady friends.

They were in luck; two Naval Reserve AD Skyraider dive bombers were scheduled to depart the base for Alameda Naval Air Station near Oakland. Since the soldiers were stationed at nearby Fort Ord, they were confident that they would make it back in time to report to the post before their weekend passes expired.

The aircraft cockpits held only one seat, which was for the pilot. There was, however, a small compartment aft in the fuselage that was normally manned by a radar operator. The radar station had a small window and

(Photofest)

The Navy AD3E "Skyraider" that was to transport Clint Eastwood from Seattle back to his California Army base during a weekend furlough. While riding in the aft radar compartment, Eastwood suddenly noticed that the plane was in trouble and losing altitude. The aircraft crashed into the sea, and the pilot and Eastwood had to swim several miles to the California shore and safety. (U.S. Navy)

was cluttered with numerous instruments and cables. The two soldiers reluctantly took passage in the claustrophobic compartments.

The taller of the two was six feet, four inches, and after being checked out on how to use an oxygen mask and the intercom, he squeezed himself into the compartment. He strapped into the operator's space and buckled his parachute.

The two aircraft took off into overcast skies and joined up to make the journey south along the Pacific coastline. The pilot in the lead was a Navy lieutenant named Anderson; his tall and lanky passenger in the rear was Pvt. Clinton Eastwood, U.S. Army Reserve.

As the plane reached altitude in cloud-filled skies, the door to Eastwood's compartment sprung open. Though he desperately tried to keep it closed, he could not get it fastened. Anderson's wingman radioed over that the door was flapping open, and try as he might, his passenger could not latch the door shut. Eastwood finally found some loose cable and managed to jury-rig the door closed.

As they flew adjacent to Medford, Oregon, the oxygen system in Anderson's plane malfunctioned. With no oxygen, the pilot radioed that he was going to land to repair the system. In attempting to stay above the overcast, Anderson climbed, and when Eastwood donned his mask, he quickly found out that he too had no oxygen. Then the intercom failed.

Eastwood now began to think about getting out of the plane. He could hear the pilot's transmissions but could not speak to him. He had noticed earlier that some cables that ran alongside him moved when Anderson closed his canopy. If they moved again, he would assume the pilot likely was bailing out. If they moved again, he was ready to follow Anderson.

Suddenly, the plane lost altitude. They had been in the air for almost three hours; Eastwood realized they were running out of fuel. As he caught a glimpse of the Golden Gate Bridge through the mist, he sighed with relief. Anderson, however, turned west and then north heading toward Point Reyes on the Marin County coast. It finally dawned on Eastwood that Anderson was going to ditch and did not want to crash-land the plane close to a populated area.

Eastwood held on as he watched the water below come closer. He felt a sudden jolt as Anderson ejected his auxiliary fuel wing tanks. The tail of the aircraft hit the water first, and after a series of hard bounces the plane came to a sudden stop and nosed down in the ocean. Eastwood quickly exited the compartment and stood on the trailing edge of the wing. Seconds later Anderson's canopy popped open and he came scrambling out of the cockpit none the worse for wear.

Point Reyes was about four miles away, and knowing that the plane would shortly sink, the two jumped into the water. The weather was still bad and the sea was rolling with high swells. They tried to stay together, but as they swam for shore the current separated them and carried them north away from their destination.

As darkness descended, Eastwood swam on alone, first through a school of jellyfish, then a kelp bed. He eventually heard surf crashing ahead, and he dimly made out large rocks along the shore taking a pounding from the onrushing water. Treading his way carefully along the shoreline and fighting a strong undertow, he finally found an opening and swam safely to the beach.

Finding no trace of Anderson along the shore, Eastwood headed for a distant light. After wading through a lagoon and climbing over a fence, he found a concrete blockhouse surrounded by antennas. The facility was an RCA relay station with a lone radio operator. Eastwood explained his situation, and the man informed him that Alameda already had aircraft in the air searching for the downed Skyraider.

The operator called the Coast Guard. They soon picked up Eastwood and brought him to the local Coast Guard station, where he was reunited with Anderson, who had drifted farther north but also made it ashore safely. The following day Eastwood was taken to the Presidio Army Base in San Francisco and informed that there would be an inquiry into the incident and that he would be called upon to testify. No investigation was held, however, and Eastwood soon was back at Fort Ord, where he reassumed his duties as a lifeguard at the base swimming pool.

Actor, film producer, and director Clint Eastwood was born on 31 May 1930 at St. Francis Hospital in San Francisco, the son of Clinton and Ruth Runer Eastwood. During the Great Depression Clint's father had difficulty finding work and the family moved often, their car pulling a one-wheeled trailer behind it. As a result of the family's nomadic lifestyle, Clint attended eight different grammar schools. An introvert who rarely enjoyed the company of other people, he did associate with a group of young men who forged a long-term loyalty among themselves. They often converged on the Eastwood household, since Clinton and Ruth were loving parents who opened their house to all. Ruth seemed always to be cooking, and free-ranging discussions on numerous subjects abounded.

Clinton finally landed a good job in a shipyard as a pipefitter, and the family settled in Oakland, California. Young Clint initially attended Piedmont High School but felt awkward and out of place with a "white bread" student body, many of whom came from wealthy families. He rebelled against the prejudices at the school, not only racial but also the bias often directed against lower-income students. He was a marginal scholar, and when he found himself ridiculed because his father worked in a shipyard, he transferred to Oakland Technical High School, where he participated in competitive swimming and basketball.

Clint also had a passion for music. By the age of fifteen he had learned to play the piano on his own, and he emulated the styles and sounds of the great musicians of the time, such as Dave Brubeck, Gerry Mulligan, Chet Baker, and Charlie Parker. His other love was cars. If you dated in Oakland, you had to have a car, and Clint had many—not fancy ones, but they were wheels. He still enjoys automobiles today, but although he has a Mercedes in his garage, he is more likely to be seen driving a pickup truck.

In 1951 during the Korean War, Clint was drafted into the Army. He never was sent to Korea but spent his two-year tour as a swimming instructor at Fort Ord, California. Several actors (Richard Long, later of *77 Sunset Strip;* Martin Milner of *Route 66;* David Janssen of *The Fugitive*) had also been inducted and spent a lot of time hanging around the pool. They suggested to the handsome swimming instructor that he ought to try acting. Though Clint did not seriously consider their chatter, he apparently was influenced by his other duties, which involved occasional teaching assignments in division classrooms. His courses included military history and recognition of military insignia. In preparing and presenting his material, he ran movie projectors and other visual aids, and this teaching experience gave him confidence in public speaking. A film that he ran often, *The Battle of San Pietro,* was a documentary produced by John Huston for the Signal Corps during World War II. Listening to the narration of the film over and over again led Eastwood to adopt Huston's cadence in a film of his own, *White Hunter, Black Heart,* many years later.

Eastwood owned a car, but because time was limited and precluded visits to San Francisco or Oakland, when he could get a pass he would drive to nearby towns. Picturesque Carmel, only twenty minutes from the base, soon became his favorite haunt. Eastwood did begin to think about living there someday, but he certainly had no clue that years later he would be elected the town's mayor.

Eastwood was discharged from the Army in 1953. Using the GI Bill entitlement, he enrolled in Los Angeles City College and majored in business administration. At the same time he began visiting studios and eventually landed a small acting contract at Universal. After months of forgettable parts in forgettable movies, he took on the role of Rowdy Yates in the CBS television series *Rawhide,* which ran from 1959 to 1966. Eastwood began to receive recognition for his cowboy portrayal in the series, but it would be nothing like what was to come.

Taking advantage of a production break in the series, Eastwood traveled to Spain in 1964 to make a "spaghetti western" directed by Sergio Leone, for which he was paid $15,000. The movie was *A Fistful of Dollars*. As "the man with no name," Eastwood became an international star in Europe. Two sequels followed—*For a Few Dollars More* and *The Good, the Bad, and the Ugly*—and his salary jumped to $250,000 per picture, plus a percentage of each movie's earnings. When the films were released in the United States in 1967, Eastwood's star began to rise. The following year United Artists gave him the lead in *Hang 'Em High,* which had very much the same look as the successful European westerns. To this day the movie remains one of the highest grossing films for the studio.

By 1969 Eastwood had become the world's top box-office draw. He began to star in movies that portrayed dimensions of the actor not seen before. In 1971, as detective Harry Callahan in *Dirty Harry,* he added a new catch phrase to America's vocabulary: "Make my day." At a time when the country was experiencing an inner-city crime wave, audiences immediately connected with a tough and unconventional police officer without qualms about taking the law into his own hands to get the job done. The sequel, *Magnum Force,* was just as popular with Eastwood fans, who did not care that critics panned both movies.

Rated number one in the Quigley Publications annual list of top ten box-office stars, Eastwood in 1972 returned to westerns in *Joe Kidd* and *High Plains Drifter.* He followed those hits with a comedy, *Thunderbolt and Lightfoot,* in 1974, and a year later an action film, *The Eiger Sanction.* Critics were beginning to see "a kind of boyish affability" in the actor, and in reference to *The Outlaw Josey Wales* (1976), a film in which Eastwood starred and also directed, "stirrings of style and humor." His work now fell into an alternating pattern of comedy and action pictures, all of which provided instant audience gratification.

In 1986 Eastwood ventured into a new career when he was elected mayor of Carmel, California. He told a reporter that he only took the job because "it's in the community where I live." His reason for running for mayor, however, was more specific and personal. He was frustrated over his unsuccessful efforts to have an abandoned building torn down next to the Hog's Breath Inn, a restaurant in Carmel of which he was part owner, in order to erect a two-story office and commercial building in its place.

Following one term in office, Eastwood returned to filmmaking. His *Bird* (1988), the story of jazz saxophonist Charlie Parker, won critical acclaim. He then directed *White Hunter, Black Heart* (1990), *The Rookie* (1991), and *Unforgiven* (1991), in which he also starred, winning Oscars for best director and best picture. Eastwood began to act in films other than his own. In 1993 he appeared as a secret service agent in *In the Line of Fire*, and that same year he teamed with Kevin Costner to costar in and direct *A Perfect World*. He also directed *The Bridges of Madison County* (1995), in which he starred with Meryl Streep, and followed that with roles in *The Stars Fell on Henrietta* (1995) and *Absolute Power* (1997). In 1998 he directed *Midnight in the Garden of Good and Evil*, and in 1999 he completed *True Crime*. Eastwood has directed and acted in more than fifty motion pictures. In addition to his Oscars, he has been honored with numerous other film awards, both within the U.S. film industry and abroad.

Eastwood married Maggie Johnson, a model, in 1953, and they had two children, Kyle and Allison. They divorced in the mid-1980s. He married his present wife, Dina Ruiz, a former television news anchor, in 1996.

Charlton Heston

O n a return flight from a movie-making venture to Russia with his wife Lydia in 1992, screen legend Charlton Heston experienced a vivid dream. It seemed that Lydia and Heston were at the Burbank Airport waiting to board an executive jet when he noticed a World War II B-17 Flying Fortress bomber parked nearby, its crew standing for a photograph. Heston approached the men and asked where they were going. One of the officers replied, "England. Eighth Air Force. Want a lift?"

Heston reluctantly declined the offer, and as the crew moved toward the aircraft, he noticed that a flight bag had been left behind. The bag was stenciled with the words, "S/SGT Heston, C. 16170644."

He suddenly understood and raced back to Lydia. He told her that he had to go, that they had a chance to do it all over again, only this

(Photofest)

time they would do it better. She said that she understood, and in a moment's flash she was eighteen again. He kissed her and ran to the plane as the number four engine roared to life. Throwing his bag into the belly of the bomber, he waved to Lydia and lifted himself up into the plane.

Once on board he noticed that the crew were all at their stations, and as he approached a waist gunner, he was startled to see himself at the age of eighteen, skinny and in uniform. The younger apparition of Heston said, "See you," and suddenly Heston was inside him. As he now looked back to where he had been previously standing, he saw no one.

To this day Heston does not know what the dream signified. He was not in the Eighth Air Force in Europe, nor did he fly in B-17s. Perhaps his dream related to his life's work. Would he want to do it all over again and perhaps do it better? Yes, like most people he would probably want to do certain things better during his life if he had another chance. But Heston decided that he wouldn't change all that had gone before. Life had been good to him, and what a life this gifted actor, artist, patriot, and highly principled man has led.

Charlton Heston was born on 4 October 1924 in Evanston, Illinois, to Lillian Charlton and Russell Whitford Carter. When Russell Carter inherited a lumber business from his father, the family moved to remote St. Helen, Michigan. With few playmates in the area, young Charlton worked for his father, and to entertain himself he turned to reading books and acting out their stories and characters. From this isolated upbringing, exacerbated by the divorce of his parents in the mid-1930s, Charlton emerged as a shy and unsophisticated young man.

Shortly after her divorce, Lillian married Chester Heston, who worked in a heating appliance plant in Wilmette, Illinois, an affluent Chicago suburb. Charlton enrolled at New Trier High School. Feeling awkward in a school that offered a host of activities, he sought to lose himself in the school's theater program and found refuge in playing many different characters in school plays. (New Trier High School produced other entertainment personalities, including Ann-Margret.)

Following graduation in 1941, Heston enrolled at nearby North-western University on a drama scholarship. In addition to appearing in numerous stage plays at both Northwestern and the Winnetka Community Theater, he was a regular on several Chicago-based radio programs. One of his most successful acting roles while at Northwestern was the lead in a production of *The American Way.* His success led to the lead role in a movie, Ibsen's *Peer Gynt,* produced by a local independent filmmaker. Though Heston had never worked in a film and knew nothing of the movie's story line, acting in the silent production was better than working in a steel mill, as he had done the summer before entering Northwestern.

With a movie behind him and the experience gained from the venture, Heston took on Northwestern with more confidence. He knew that he had found his calling and was convinced that he would be given any part he read for. Although that was not the case, it did not stop his growing ambition. Northwestern offered then and still does today one of the best theater departments in the country (among its products are Robert Goulet, Glenn Close, Carol Lawrence, and Patricia Neal). Heston relished the drama classes he was able to take in addition to his required liberal arts courses. It was also at Northwestern that Heston met Lydia Clarke, "the lodestone of my life, the girl who married me."

Heston fell in love with Lydia at first sight. They shared classes and acted in several stage productions together. Then, on 7 December 1941, the Japanese attacked Pearl Harbor, and like all Americans, Heston shared the national outrage that swept across the country. He enlisted in the Army Air Corps but was not called up until six months later. During that time he continued his studies, worked part time as an elevator man in an apartment building on Lake Michigan, and continued his relentless marriage quest of Lydia. But she was determined to get her degree, and although she became his "girl," she would not accept his proposal.

In June 1941 Heston reported for basic training at a temporary camp outside of Greensboro, North Carolina. His initial letters to Lydia continued to mention marriage, but the grind of his schedule eventually led him to give up that hope. Nevertheless, toward the end of his training Heston received a letter from her: "Have decided to accept your proposal. Love, Lydia." She shortly thereafter came to Greensboro, and they were married. Their marriage endures to this day, nearly sixty years later.

Lydia returned to Northwestern, and Heston was sent on to radio school and then aerial gunnery training, shuttling between Scott Field,

Illinois; Shepard Field, Texas; and Selfridge Field, Michigan. Selfridge, located near Detroit, was a short distance from Chicago, and Charlton and Lydia were able to spend time together before he shipped out.

By now a sergeant, Heston and his classmates were convinced that they were headed for the China-Burma-India theater. They received shots for the region, drew tropical uniforms, and watched films that dealt with troopship discipline over extended ocean voyages.

In mid-1944 Heston was a member of a flight crew and was in Seattle awaiting orders and transportation. One night after lights out, the men in Heston's crew, along with members of some twenty other crews, were awakened to board a civilian passenger ship that had been commandeered by the Army to transport them to Alaska. In June 1942 the Japanese had occupied two of the American Aleutian Islands, Kiska and Attu. Nearly a year later, in May 1943, three thousand troops of the 7th U.S. Infantry Division invaded the north and south coasts of Attu. On 29 May a thousand Japanese soldiers descended silently from the mountains and attacked the Americans. Before the Japanese troops could be stopped, they overran two command posts and broke into a medical station, killing all the sick and wounded. As they were brought to bay, five hundred of the attackers committed suicide with hand grenades. Twenty-eight captives were taken and the rest were killed. It took eleven thousand American soldiers to eventually drive out the Japanese defenders, many holed up in mountain caves. When Attu was finally secured, the Japanese had suffered more than two thousand killed. American losses were six hundred dead and twelve hundred wounded.

Three months later, twenty-nine thousand U.S. and fifty-three hundred Canadian troops landed on Kiska. The invaders found the island unoccupied. Japanese cruisers and destroyers had evacuated the entire Japanese garrison three weeks earlier.

American intelligence believed that the Japanese would return to the islands, and the air crewmen who sailed on board Heston's liner were hastened north to reinforce the U.S. Eleventh Air Force with its numerous bases positioned along the Aleutian chain. Heston joined the 77th Bombardment Squadron on Attu. He was assigned to a B-25 Billy Mitchell medium bomber crew as radioman and gunner.

The 77th conducted combat operations in the North Pacific from February 1942 to July 1945. The squadron was awarded a Distin-

Charlton Heston enlisted in the AAF in 1942 and served with the 77th Bombardment Squadron, Eleventh Air Force, in the Aleutians during World War II. Shown are squadron B-25 Billy Mitchell medium bombers en route to targets in enemy-held territory. Heston was honorably discharged in 1945. (U.S. Air Force)

guished Unit Citation for its Kuril Islands operations between April 1944 and July 1945.

In September 1943 the 77th Bombardment Squadron had participated in the historic Paramushiro operation, attacking the Japanese naval base in a series of harassment raids. The campaign, however, proved ineffective and was abandoned. The 77th regularly flew anti-shipping patrols in weather conditions that were at best hazardous and often extremely dangerous. The average wind factor at Attu was thirty-two miles per hour, and if a crew lived through a crash into the ocean, the airmen were lucky if they survived for five minutes in the frigid Alaskan waters. Flights frequently were canceled because of snow, fog, and freezing rain.

Heston spent the remainder of the war on a treeless island with one volcano whose crater was garnished with orchids. The chances of an enemy amphibious operation against the islands were nil, and with no diversions, tension among personnel was an ongoing problem. In that environment Heston got into the last fistfight of his life, and it was over a game of chess. There were positive distractions, however, when herds of caribou wandered near the base. Fresh meat was always welcome.

Heston's Aleutian duty ended when one of the squadron bombers crashed while trying to land in a forty-mile-an-hour crosswind. While racing toward the plane to help, he slipped on the ice and slid under an ambulance. He was picked up with the survivors of the crash, awoke in a plaster cast, and was flown to a stateside hospital. Once recovered, he found himself grounded and running the control tower at Elmendorf Air Base in Anchorage, Alaska.

The war, however, was not over for Heston. The Allies were planning the invasion of the Japanese home islands, a daunting task that promised extraordinary casualties on both sides. Operation Downfall, which called for two assaults, was to commence in November 1945. The first attack, Operation Olympic, was planned for 1 November and targeted the southern island of Kyushu. That was to be followed in the spring of 1946 by Operation Coronet, an air and ground attack on the northernmost Japanese island of Hokkaido, and on Tokyo on the main island of Honshu with the objective of capturing the military government and the emperor. The U.S. Eighth Army and First Army were to commence the Tokyo plan on 1 March. The Eleventh Air Force, to which Heston was still attached, would go to Okinawa to prepare for action in both operations. Heston was likely to be back in the air on board a B-25 bomber.

On 6 August 1945 the world's first atomic bomb was dropped on Hiroshima. It practically obliterated the city. Three days later another bomb was dropped on Nagasaki. On 15 August Allied commands ordered a cease-fire; Japan had surrendered. The formal signing of the instrument of surrender took place on 2 September 1945 on board the U.S. battleship *Missouri* in Tokyo Bay. Supreme Commander of the Allied Forces, Gen. Douglas MacArthur, ended the ceremony with the words "Let us pray that peace be now restored to the world and that God will preserve it always. These proceedings now are closed."

Sergeant Heston received his orders to return home in March 1946. Before he departed, however, there was a slight hitch. In his exuberance he lost control of his jeep on an icy road and piled it into a snow-bank. He was not hurt, nor was the jeep, but he was worried that someone might have seen the incident and that he would be delayed for further inspection. So he took a chance and did not mention it when he checked the vehicle in to squadron inventory. Then, strapped in his seat in the plane, he sweated out the moments until the aircraft at last lifted off. Later, while over Canada, the plane lost two of its four engines, but it landed safely in Great Falls, Montana, where Heston was processed out of the Army.

Heston and his wife both found work in Chicago, but they eventu-ally moved to New York. Acting jobs were few and far between on or off Broadway at the time, so they joined the Thomas Wolfe Memorial Theatre in Asheville, North Carolina, as codirectors and leading play-ers. After several months they returned to New York, where Heston was selected for the role of Proculeius, Caesar's lieutenant, in Kather-ine Cornell's stage play *Antony and Cleopatra*, which opened for a seven-month run on Broadway in November 1947. Over the next three years he found steady stage work, but the most promising employment opportunities for young actors not tied to movie studio contracts (which disallowed TV appearances) were in the fast-emerging televi-sion industry.

Though the money was minuscule (Heston was paid sixty-eight dol-lars for his first *Studio One* appearance), plenty of work was avail-able for actors like Charlton Heston on TV programs such as *Philco Playhouse, Omnibus, Robert Montgomery Presents, Curtain Call,* and *Studio One.*

Impressed with Heston's acting talent, motion picture producer Hal Wallis signed him to a long-term film contract in 1950. Heston made his screen debut the following year in *Dark City* and received favorable reviews from movie critics. Over the next few years he played a variety of roles, but none that established him as a ranking star. It was not until 1956, when Cecil B. DeMille cast him as Moses in *The Ten Com-mandments,* that Heston was recognized as a major screen talent. Four years later he won an Academy Award as best actor for his role in the biblical spectacular *Ben Hur.* (In 1978 he gathered another Oscar, the Jean Hersholt Humanitarian Award.) He went on to play larger-than-life historical figures, such as Andrew Jackson in *The President's Lady*

(1953), Michelangelo in *The Agony and the Ecstasy* (1965), British general Charles "Chinese" Gordon in *Khartoum* (1966), Marc Antony in *Julius Caesar* (1970), and Cardinal Richelieu in *The Three Musketeers* (1974). He has appeared in more than seventy films over the past fifty years.

In 1963 Heston was elected president of the Screen Actors Guild (the actors union), a post he held until 1975. During his tenure he became active in the civil rights movement. He participated in various protest marches, and along with Burt Lancaster, James Garner, Marlon Brando, Paul Newman, Sidney Poitier, and Harry Belafonte, he walked behind Dr. Martin Luther King in the famous March on Washington in 1963. These actors believed deeply in their convictions, and their presence with Dr. King raised the public's awareness of the civil rights issue. In 1964 President Lyndon Johnson persuaded Congress to enact the Civil Rights Act. Heston still takes great pride in having played a part in that movement.

Ever the patriot, Heston decided to visit Vietnam in the mid-1960s during that controversial war. He flew to Saigon in 1966 and met with troops in Danang, Pleiku, and forward positions such as Ba To, Gia Phuc, Tra Bong, La Hai, Me Thout, and Dong Tre. After his Pleiku visit he spent some time with the Montagnards and was initiated into their tribe. Two years later he returned to the war-torn country. He revisited some of the camps he had gone to during his initial tour and this time added a few more, such as the An Khe Valley, Luach, and Tanan. As before, he flew into the Green Beret base in Montagnard country and endured ritual eating ceremonies with his native hosts, which played havoc with his digestive system. In the fall of 1983 Heston visited with U.S. troops in Beruit following the destruction of the Marine barracks by terrorists, which left 241 Marines dead.

In 1993 Heston flew to Somalia to meet with Army and Marine units deployed in peacekeeping operations. He visited a Catholic orphanage and the Royal Australia Regiment in Bardera. He talked with many of the Aussies and discovered that although they were glad to be there, they felt that they were involved in an impossible task because of the strict ground rules. The Australians left a month later. American troops stayed until the fall, when they were compelled to abandon the mission following serious personnel losses.

During his professional life Charlton Heston has served his fellow artists well. In addition to his twelve-year term as president of the Screen Actors Guild, he served as chairman of the Board of Trustees of the American Film Institute, a nonprofit organization established by the National Endowment for the Arts in the 1960s to preserve America's film heritage and train new filmmakers. Heston also sat on the National Council of the Arts from 1966 to 1972, and in 1981 President Ronald Reagan chose him to cochair the White House Task Force on the Arts and Humanities.

As of this writing Charlton Heston continues to work at his profession, write books, enthusiastically stump for political candidates, and articulate with passion his deeply felt beliefs on public issues. His strong commitment to the Second Amendment led him in the spring of 1998 to assume the presidency of the National Rifle Association. In the same year his seventy-fifth movie, *Town and Country,* was shot. He is considered by many to be the elder statesman of Hollywood. His autobiography, *In the Arena,* published in 1995, quotes the following passage by Theodore Roosevelt. It perhaps best describes Charlton Heston's philosophy of life:

> It is not the critic who counts, not the man who points out where the strong stumbled, or how the doer could have done better. The credit belongs to the man who is in the arena, his face marred by dust and sweat and blood, who strives valiantly, who errs and falls short again and again; there is no effort without error.

> But he who tries, who knows the great enthusiasms, the great devotions, who spends himself in a worthy cause, at best knows the triumph of achievement, and at worst, fails while daring. His place shall never be with those cold and timid souls who knew neither victory nor defeat.

William Holden

On the closing pages of James Michener's novel *The Bridges at Toko-Ri*, Admiral Tarrant, commander Task Force 77, is informed of the loss of one of his pilots, Lieutenant Brubaker, after his jet fighter has crashed during a raid on the Toko-Ri bridges in North Korea. Brubaker was a favorite of the admiral, and he mourned his loss. Thinking of Brubaker and the other pilots who flew from his carrier, the *Savo*, Tarrant asks, "Why is America lucky enough to have such men? They leave this tiny ship and fly against the enemy. Then they must seek the ship, lost somewhere on the sea. And when they find it, they have to land upon its pitching deck. Where did we get such men?"

In the 1954 movie made from Michener's novel, the admiral was played by Frederic March and the pilot by William Holden. It was ironic that Holden should play a role that paralleled the loss of his

(Photofest)

brother, Bob, who was shot down and killed by Japanese Zeroes off Kavieng, New Ireland, some ten years earlier. And that was not the last family tragedy suffered by Holden's family from an air mishap. His only other brother, Dick, a former Air Force pilot, was lost in the 1960s while piloting a light plane over Peru on family company business.

One of Hollywood's most enduring actors, William Holden was born William Franklin Beedle, Jr., on 17 April 1918 at O'Fallon, Illinois, a small town some twenty miles from St. Louis, Missouri. Billy moved to California with his parents, Mary and William, and his younger brother, Bob, in the early 1920s. William Beedle, a chemist, found work at the George W. Gooch Laboratories, where he eventually became head of the company.

Billy attended school in Monrovia and South Pasadena and then enrolled at South Pasadena College. He was a handsome young man who lived life on the edge, riding motorcycles and driving cars at break-neck speeds—a habit that stayed with him throughout his life. A less-than-average student in college, he excelled in gymnastics, sang in an a cappella choir, and took an interest in theater, studying radio drama and acting in numerous radio plays.

After appearing in a play at the Playhouse Theater, Billy Beedle was noticed by a talent scout, given a screen test, and signed by Paramount Studios. On 22 February 1939, a short piece in the *Los Angeles Times* noted:

> Another Juvenile find is registered. Paramount has signed one William Beedle (20 years of age) and changed his name to William Holden.
>
> The new discovery, a student of Pasadena Junior College, is considered very promising and has been cast importantly in "What a Life," the Jackie Cooper feature.

Holden did not work in Cooper's film; it was merely the studio's method for getting the title of a new picture into print.

Holden seemed destined for stardom. Columbia Pictures at the time was looking for a lead actor to play in the film *Golden Boy*. John Garfield would have been the ideal choice, but at the time he was under contract with Warner Brothers and they would not let him play the part. *Golden Boy* was the story of a gifted young man who struggled between two loves in his life, prizefighting and playing the violin. When no major name was available, Bill Holden was cast in the role. The film made him an overnight star.

Among the prominent cast members was Barbara Stanwyck, who worked with the young, very nervous, and inexperienced actor until he was able to give a credible performance. Holden never forgot her generosity, and throughout the rest of his life he called her "Queen"; she called him "Golden Boy." Receiving critical acclaim for his performance, he was cast in a number of subsequent roles requiring a clean-cut leading man. During the next several years he appeared in *Invisible Man* (1939), *Our Town* and *Arizona* (1940), *I Wanted Wings* and *Texas* (1941), and *The Remarkable Andrew, Meet the Stewarts,* and *The Fleet's In* (all in 1942). His last film before joining the Army was *Young and Willing* (1943).

While Holden was making *Invisible Stripes* (1940), a beautiful young actress by the name of Brenda Marshall (the former Ardis Ankerson) walked onto the set. Holden became entranced, and after a tumultuous courtship they married. A few weeks later Holden decided to volunteer for military service. His brother Bob was in the Navy, and America was fully engaged in World War II.

On 20 April 1942 Bill Holden was sworn into the Army at the Los Angeles recruiting station on Main Street. After reporting to Fort MacArthur Reception Center, he was shipped off to Tarrant Field Air Base near Fort Worth, Texas. Private Beedle was then ordered to Fort Monmouth, New Jersey, for basic training with the Signal Corps. He subsequently qualified for officer training and was commissioned a second lieutenant in the AAF on 20 January 1943. He returned to Tarrant, where he reported to the First Motion Picture Unit Training Command. His roommate was baseball star Hank Greenberg.

Although Holden repeatedly requested combat duty, he was assigned to a public relations billet. Like Navy lieutenant Robert Taylor, another established Hollywood star, Holden appeared in training films and on various radio shows promoting the nation's war effort. His brother Bob was in Texas at the same time undergoing Navy flight training. Although they corresponded frequently, they could never rendezvous because of conflicting schedules. Holden often regretted this after his brother was lost in the Pacific the following January.

Lt. Willam Holden, AAF, takes a dining break at Sherman Billingsley's Stork Club in New York while on a July 1944 bond tour from his station in Fort Worth, Texas. Holden's brother, a Navy pilot, was lost during the war. (Photofest)

He had a premonition of Bob's loss on New Year's Day 1944, when he awoke in his quarters at Fort Worth visibly distraught. He phoned his wife and was assured that everything was fine at home. He then called his parents in Pasadena, asking questions about their welfare. They too were in good spirits. For the next few days, however, Holden could not shake a feeling of depression. On 4 January 1944 his parents received word that Bob had been killed in action on a combat mission on New Year's Day. Holden shared his sorrow with no one. He felt that he had failed Bob, and in the process himself, by not staying in closer touch with his brother.

In 1945 Holden was ordered to the First Motion Picture Unit at the Hal Roach Studios. He arrived at Fort Roach with a friend, Richard Webb, and they reported to the adjutant's office to present their credentials. They remained at attention for twenty-five minutes while the officer proceeded to recite base and unit regulations meticulously. That adjutant was Capt. Ronald Reagan.

After more than three years of service, William Holden was discharged from the Army in September 1945. Though he had continually requested combat duty, he was turned down time and again by higher authorities who determined that he would be of more value to the war effort by staying in the States and making training and morale-boosting films. He readily joined war-bond rallies, appeared as a guest on talent shows, and was warm and accessible to both military and civilian personnel he encountered. Like many established stars who joined the military during the war, he faced resentment from some career military personnel who would give no quarter to movie stars. Movie celebrities such as Holden worked as hard as others who served during the war. He never requested special treatment. He was dedicated to serving his country and did so honorably.

After his discharge, Holden returned to Columbia Studios, where for about a year he found work very scarce. Then fortune struck and he was cast in numerous quality films over the next several years. Memorable movies in which he appeared in the 1950s include *Sunset Boulevard* (1950), for which he was nominated for an Academy Award; *Born Yesterday* (1950); *The Moon Is Blue* (1953); *Stalag 17* (1953), for which he won the Academy of Motion Picture Arts and Sciences Award as the best male actor of 1953; and *Executive Suite*, *Sabrina*, *The Country Girl*, and *The Bridges at Toko-Ri*, all produced in 1954. Those were shortly followed by *Love Is a Many Splendored Thing* and *Picnic*, which both premiered in 1955. In 1957 Holden appeared with Alec Guiness in *The Bridge on the River Kwai*.

Holden loved to travel and at one time lived in Switzerland. He was enchanted with Africa and spent much of his time in Kenya, where he was part owner of a country club. Unfortunately, he had a serious drinking problem, one which had begun while he was stationed at Fort Worth during the war. With little to do and facing fierce heat and blowing dust every day, he and his roommate, Hank Greenberg, "would go out and get drunk every night." Drinking became a habit for Holden and, indeed, he suffered from alcoholism for a good part of his professional career. Although he made a heroic effort to overcome the addiction, he was never able to master his drinking problem. After thirty years of marriage, he and Ardis divorced. Holden never remarried, although he and actress Stefanie Powers (of *Hart to Hart* TV fame) were seriously involved for a number of years. They shared a love of the African wilderness and spent considerable time there.

On 16 November 1981 police found the actor dead in his apartment, alone. It appeared that he had been drinking and slipped on a throw rug, falling and hitting his head on a sharp corner of a bedside table. William Holden bled to death. He was sixty-three years old.

David Ansen in *Newsweek* noted how Holden's good looks made him a star in *Golden Boy*. "But," the critic went on, "the beauty was moral, too; the mature Holden re-emerged with ravaged stoicism in *The Wild Bunch* and became a symbol of hard bitten decency in *Network* and *S.O.B.* He was courtly, cynical, possessed of a particularly American gallantry that was utterly free of airs."

At the 1982 Academy Awards ceremony John Travolta recalled an incident that had occurred four years earlier, when Bill Holden was an awards presenter along with actress Barbara Stanwyck. Holden had departed from the script during their segment of the program to pay tribute to the lady standing next to him. He stated that he owed his career to Ms. Stanwyck and that what he had become as an actor stemmed from her generosity, support, and belief in him.

Travolta then presented Stanwyck with the academy's honorary award for her many accomplishments. Upon a standing ovation from the audience, she finished her remarks with the following words: "A few years ago, I stood on this stage with William Holden as a presenter. I loved him very much and I miss him. He always wished I would get an Oscar. And so tonight, my Golden Boy, you got your wish."

Burt Lancaster

When Burt Lancaster passed away in 1994 at the age of eighty-one, he was regarded as one of the finest actors Hollywood has ever produced. His achievements included a best actor Oscar, a Golden Globe Award, and the New York Film Critics Award, all for his portrayal of an intense revival preacher in *Elmer Gantry* (1960). He also received Academy Award nominations for *From Here to Eternity* (1953), *Birdman of Alcatraz* (1962), and *Atlantic City* (1980).

As a young man Burt Lancaster possessed a dazzling smile, sharp, bold features, and a trim and athletic body. He had a commanding presence, and when he entered a room, people sensed an air of electricity around him.

Lancaster was a versatile actor who often sought offbeat and challenging roles. He seemed to relish risk, taking parts that other actors

(Photofest)

would decline. He chose impassioned films about the underdogs of life—the poor, the oppressed, the victims of prejudice.

Born Burton Stephen Lancaster on 2 November 1913 in New York City, Lancaster grew up in the tough East Harlem section of Manhattan's Upper East Side. He was an exceptional athlete at DeWitt Clinton High School and was awarded an athletic scholarship to New York University. A physical education major at NYU, he played on the school's basketball and baseball teams, ran track, and was a superb gymnast.

Lancaster left college after two years and teamed up with a boyhood friend, Nick Cravat, to develop an acrobatic routine. "Lang and Cravat" joined the Kay Brothers Circus, worked for thirty weeks, then joined another circus. Between 1932 and 1939 the two worked in vaudeville shows, carnivals, and circuses. At one point they were a featured act with Ringling Brothers.

Due to an infected thumb, Lancaster had to give up acrobatics. To make ends meet he took on a variety of jobs, including floor walker in the lingerie department of Marshall Field's store in Chicago, salesman in the store's haberdashery department, and fireman and engineer for a Chicago meat-packing plant.

Upon returning to New York in 1942 to consider a position with the Columbia Concerts Bureau of CBS radio, Lancaster learned he was about to be drafted. He was inducted into the Army on 2 January 1943, and his professional life was put on hold. He had hopes that because of his experience as a circus rigger he would be assigned to the Engineering Corps. Instead, he was sent to the 21st Special Services Unit, whose mission was to entertain troops. By 11 January, 102 enlisted men had joined the unit.

Assigned as an athletics instructor, Lancaster organized teams, refereed boxing matches, and scheduled and participated in general fitness programs. He was promoted to corporal (Tech 5) in April 1943 as the unit was moved to Camp Sibert, Alabama.

Following Operation Torch, the invasion of North Africa in 1942, and subsequent victory over Axis forces there in 1943, the 21st was attached to Gen. Mark Clark's Fifth Army and sent to Africa to entertain the thousands of Allied soldiers who occupied the newly won territory. The unit's first show, *Let's Go,* was performed in Casablanca. In September 1943

Burt Lancaster was drafted into the Army in 1942 and assigned to the
21st Special Services Unit of the Fifth Army as an entertainer. (Prior to
his service, he had performed in a circus.) Lancaster ended up organizing and directing shows and was sent overseas. One of his productions,
Stars and Gripes, was performed in North Africa, Sicily, Italy, and Austria. He was honorably discharged in 1945. (Photofest)

they were stationed at Bizerte, Tunisia, where they debuted a new show,
Stars and Gripes. When the unit arrived overseas, Lancaster had been
reassigned as an entertainment specialist. In his new role he directed,
wrote skits, and performed in *Stars and Gripes*, although he later complained that he was no more than a pianist's page turner.

Stars and Gripes turned into a success, and some ninety performances were given in Algiers between September and Thanksgiving 1943 to a total of seventy-five thousand GIs. The 21st continued to perform, following Clark's Fifth Army as it moved up the Italian boot. The Fifth reached Naples on 1 October, and although the Italians had surrendered the previous September, there were still German forces to battle. Lancaster often commented that although their show was frequently interrupted by gunfire, they were in no immediate danger. It was routine, however, to hear guns booming at the front lines as actors delivered their lines and comedians told jokes.

Stars and Gripes was the first live show to be performed at Anzio, and it was also the first to be staged in Rome. In late 1944 the 21st Special Services Unit settled down in the city of Montecatini, just northwest of Florence. With its numerous theaters, spacious spa, sports center, and two libraries, it was a perfect rest center for the Fifth Army. The 21st accommodated some twenty thousand GIs a day. It also hosted the numerous USO camp shows that passed through the area. It was there that Lancaster met his future wife, Norma Mari Anderson, a native of Webster, Wisconsin. When she encountered Lancaster she was on a solo junket with a USO show, having volunteered to take the place of a chorus girl who had fallen sick. They met, fell in love, and parted, hoping to continue their romance after the war.

When Germany surrendered, Lancaster was in Modena, north of Montecatini, where their show was playing. He stayed in Italy until June, when the 21st was loaded on a ship destined for the Pacific theater via the States. When the ship finally docked at Hampton Roads, Virginia, the Japanese were on board the USS *Missouri* signing surrender documents. The war was over. Upon being honorably discharged from the Army at Fort Dix in New Jersey after two years and nine months, Tech 5 Lancaster had been awarded the Good Conduct Medal, the American Campaign Medal, the European–African–Middle Eastern Campaign Medal with four bronze star devices (Naples-Foggia, North Apennines, Po Valley, Rome-Arno), the World War II Victory Medal, and four overseas service bars.

During an extended furlough prior to his discharge, Lancaster took the opportunity to visit Norma Anderson, who was working at ABC radio in New York. He was still in uniform when he entered the RCA

Building (the location of ABC radio), and while riding up on the elevator he was approached by a talent scout named Jack Mahlor. Mahlor explained that he was looking for people to fit certain theatrical roles, and Lancaster was invited to read for a play, *A Sound of Hunting*. He got the part and, although the play ran for only three weeks, it was enough to bring him to the attention of Hollywood scouts.

Lancaster soon found himself cast in the movie *The Killers* (1946), which immediately established him as a star. During his long and illustrious film career, Burt Lancaster appeared in more than seventy-five films. He married three times; Norma Anderson was his second wife. His marriages produced two sons and three daughters. As late as 1990 he finished a highly acclaimed television movie, *Separate but Equal*. It was to be his last performance. He suffered a massive stroke shortly thereafter and never worked again. Burt Lancaster died in 1994. Some of his other films were *Gunfight at the O.K. Corral* (1957), *Run Silent, Run Deep* (1958), *Seven Days in May* (1964), *Airport* (1970), and *Field of Dreams* (1989).

Glenn Miller

Glenn Miller's band may possibly be remembered as the most popular orchestra of the twentieth century. Miller was arguably the most successful bandleader in an era itself often characterized by the many big bands that competed in clubs, concerts, over the airwaves, and on recordings for the attention and loyalty of America's youth. Even today, there are few who do not instantly recognize the Miller sound, a sound so unique that it took the country by storm in the late 1930s and several years later became identified forever with World War II and the generation that fought it.

Alton Glenn Miller was born in the small southwest Iowa town of Clarinda in 1904, attended the University of Colorado, and joined the Ben Pollack Band as a trombonist in 1926. He later became a freelance musician and organizer of other bands, namely, the Dorsey brothers

(U.S. Air Force)

(1934) and Ray Noble (1935). Although his first effort to form his own orchestra failed, his second attempt exceeded his own and the music world's expectations.

When Glenn Miller put together his second band, he decided not to follow the swing bands of Artie Shaw, Benny Goodman, and the Dorseys. Instead he strove for a sweet-sounding band with an identifiable style, but one that could also swing for a youthful audience. Miller found his unique sound by emphasizing his reed section. Contrary to the idea conveyed in the movie *The Glenn Miller Story* (1954), the Miller sound did not result from the split lip of one of his trumpet players and the replacement of that instrument by a clarinet in subsequent arrangements. The true discovery of the Miller sound was made by accident.

During his days with the Ray Noble Band, Peewee Erwin, who was playing trumpet, asked the group's arranger, who happened to be Glenn Miller, for high parts on his horn. Miller complied and wrote compositions for Peewee with saxes playing underneath. When Erwin left the band, Miller later remembered, his replacement could not hit the high notes, so they decided to assign the B-flat trumpet parts to a B-flat clarinet and double the clarinet with tenor saxes playing an octave lower. And that was how the Miller style began.

This truly unique approach, of course, required Miller arrangements and a band that could play with a sweeping legato style. Through meticulous selection of new musicians, Miller put together a band that captured the magic of these new arrangements. Miller introduced his new sound on 16 April 1938, when he opened at the Raymor Ballroom in Boston. George T. Simon (later Miller's biographer) wrote at the time in *Metronome:* "Note, for example, his unique style of scoring for one clarinet and four saxes, and then some of the moving background figures he writes for the brass to play into hats, and you'll get a pretty good idea of the swell, set style upon which he and his men are working." Glenn Miller's star began to rise, and soon his recorded and broadcast renditions of "Moonlight Serenade," "In the Mood," "I've Got a Gal in Kalamazoo," "Little Brown Jug," and "Pennsylvania 6–5000" were playing across America. The Glenn Miller Band reached the hearts of music lovers as no other band had done before.

When America went to war in 1941, Glenn Miller was at the height of his popularity. The band was in demand from coast to coast, and its

A famed bandleader before World War II, Glenn Miller disbanded his orchestra when the war started and joined the Army in 1942. He was initially commissioned a captain and then promoted to major after transferring to the AAF. He assembled an AAF band made up of many of the nation's best musicians then in uniform and took the band to England, where it made numerous appearances and a series of superb recordings. Tragically, Miller was lost when his small plane disappeared mysteriously over the English Channel on 15 December 1944. Miller is shown here with musicians Ray McKinley and Mel Powell. (Photofest)

success was further enhanced by appearances in two movies, *Sun Valley Serenade* (1941) and *Orchestra Wives* (1942). In the spring of 1942 the draft started to have an impact on dance bands. Miller was an ardent patriot, and he began to think about the morale needs of the thousands of America's young men in training camps. He initiated a radio program called *Sunset Serenade* dedicated to the country's servicemen who were readying themselves for war at bases across America.

Carrying his dedication to the cause a step further, on 20 June 1942 Miller applied for a commission in the Naval Reserve. His application was accompanied by an accounting of his business and professional experience as well as personal references, one of which was a flattering letter from Bing Crosby. On 1 August 1942 Miller received a letter from the chief of Navy personnel:

> You are advised that, after careful consideration, the Bureau is unable to approve your application for appointment in the U.S. Naval Reserve for the reason or reasons indicated below:
>
> You have not established to the satisfaction of the Navy Department that your particular qualifications fit you for a mobilizations billet in the Naval Reserve.

The Navy would later be sorry about that decision.

Stung by the Navy's rebuff, Miller fired off a letter to his Army friend Gen. Charles D. Young in which he proposed to form a first-rate Army band. The idea of a large, modernized Army band appealed to General Young, and if Miller, as he stated in his return letter, was ready to sign on for the duration, the Army would benefit greatly from bringing him on board. Thirty-eight-year-old Miller was invited to Washington, D.C., where he filed his official application, passed an Army physical, and was offered a captain's reserve commission.

Glenn was assigned immediately to the Army Specialists Corps following his induction in New York City on 7 October 1942. He went through basic training just like all recruits. And although he did not cotton to the pushups, marching drills, target practice, and other military duties, he was learning how to take orders. This was clearly different from what he had been used to as a renowned civilian band leader.

Glenn Miller's first duty station was the Seventh Command Headquarters in Omaha, Nebraska. Shortly thereafter, he was transferred to Fort Meade, Maryland, for officers' training; he was commissioned there as a captain in the United States Army Reserve on 4 December 1942. Ordered back to Omaha, he was abruptly transferred to the Army Air Forces and sent to Maxwell Field, Alabama, and an assignment as assistant special services officer. Miller soon found himself at the Army Air Forces Technical Training Command at Knollwood Field, North Carolina.

In retrospect it appeared that the Army Air Corps had pulled off a coup in acquiring Miller. Evidently the Army did not realize that it had *the* Glenn Miller in its ranks, just someone named Alton G. Miller. A shrewd AAF officer discovered Miller's real first name, just who this freshly minted officer was, and through a simple request was able to have him routinely moved out of the ground forces and into the air arm. The Navy and old Army had now both lost out on the services of the famed band leader, and the Air Corps would forever count its good fortune.

In his new position Miller hoped to create a number of new AAF bands that could perform dance band tunes as well as the more typical military standards. He took his job as a morale builder seriously, and he felt he knew as well as anyone the kind of music young soldiers and airmen most wanted to hear. But road blocks were set up immediately by senior officers who were resistant to change and resented anyone who might challenge their authority. They preferred the time-honored martial music written by military composers such as John Philip Sousa. Nothing would change on their watch. Miller was devastated by this turn of events, but there was little he could do. He managed to salvage one aspect of his plan, which was to organize one absolutely first-rate band. Eventually he was appointed director of bands training for the Army Air Forces Technical Training Command.

Glenn Miller began to form his band by gathering old hands from his civilian band who had been drafted and by adding new, highly talented musicians. He trained his new band, the 418th Army Air Forces Band, at Yale University in New Haven, Connecticut. A large portion of Yale had been turned into an Air Force cadets' training center, and the band during its early days played music in the Glenn Miller style for parade reviews, evening retreat, and during lunch hours. It was during that time that the Glenn Miller AAF Band came up with its famous marching arrangement of the "St. Louis Blues." Martial versions of "Blues in the Night" and "Jersey Bounce" followed, and the marching cadets soon had a swing in their step.

In mid-1943 Miller inaugurated a weekly radio series called *I Sustain the Wings*. By July the show was being broadcast nationwide, first on CBS and then on NBC. Its purpose was to promote the AAF and recruit young men into the service. The band made broadcasts for the Treasury Department and programs called *Uncle Sam Presents*. It also recorded V-Discs that were played in camps around the world. The Air Force eventually began to appreciate the morale and recruiting value of the *Wings* show and relieved Miller of his training command duties so that he could concentrate on the program. Nevertheless, Miller still had to answer to nervous top brass in the Pentagon and the harassment continued, especially after he presented his innovative marching band in July in the Yale Bowl.

Glenn's growing ambition was to take his band to Europe and play for the GIs. Paving the way for that move, the band on 30 April 1944 became the 2001st Base Unit (Radio Production) with all of its men assigned to Captain Miller's control. They would no longer be under the auspices of the Headquarters Detachment at Yale. By late May the word was out that Glenn Miller's AAF Band was going overseas. On 21 June 1944 the sixty-two-member band boarded the *Queen Mary* destined for Scotland's Firth of Clyde.

When the band arrived they found England in the midst of a German Buzz Bomb blitz. The musicians were initially housed at 25 Sloane Court in London. Most of the bombs seemed to fly directly over the quarters, and the area became known as Buzz Bomb Alley. Rather than taking to shelters, a few of the musicians, including vocalist Johnny Desmond, took to the roof of the building to watch the streaking missiles. They felt that if they could see the weapons they could not be hurt. In addition, they did not much care for the foul air in the bomb shelters. Concerned for the safety of his men, Miller received permission to move them to Bedford, some fifty miles north of London. There they converted a temporary BBC studio into one that was suitable for music.

A week after they arrived in England the band broadcast its first program over the Allied Expeditionary Forces Network and the BBC, England's sole network. The American brass in Europe were delighted to have the Miller band under their jurisdiction and renamed the group Captain Glenn Miller and his American Band of the Supreme Allied Command. During its five-and-a-half-month stay in England, Glenn Miller's orchestra played seventy-one concerts before approximately 248,000 enthusiastic listeners. The Miller group gained many new, ardent fans, among them the Queen of England and Gen. Dwight D. Eisenhower, supreme commander of the Allied Expeditionary Forces in Western Europe. Perhaps James Doolittle, commander of the Eighth Army Air Force, summed it up best when he said, "Captain Miller, next to a letter from home your organization is the greatest morale-builder in the European Theater of Operations."

Miller was promoted to major effective 17 August 1944. The band's popularity continued to grow, and demands in England for appearances increased. The musicians kept up an exhausting schedule, attempting to meet the many camp show requests while continuing to produce radio broadcasts. During that period Miller and his band recorded six propaganda programs called *Music for the Wehrmacht,* which were played from underground studios of the American Broadcasting Station in Europe on Wardour Street in London. Since Allied forces were advancing rapidly on the Continent, it was hoped that the Miller sound might be additional evidence to the German troops that the war's outcome was inevitable and they would be better off to end it as soon as possible.

The announcer for the programs was German-speaking Ilse Weinberger; she was joined by Herr Major Miller speaking awkwardly in phonetic German (providing his colleagues endless amusement), and Sgt. Johnny Desmond and Artie Malvin, who provided the vocals, singing in German. Typically, they started with "In the Mood" and moved on to "Stardust" and other big band classics. The dialogue during the programs focused on music and its universality for all people, regardless of political borders, and of course the freedom of Americans to listen to whatever they chose (jazz and other popular music had been banned in Germany much earlier). These programs began broadcasting on Wednesdays in early November 1944. It was later learned that despite German jamming efforts, much of the programming got through to the German population, including the troops. The programs survived the war and are available today.

On 15 November Miller was summoned to SHAEF at Versailles. Paris had been liberated and Miller was asked if he would like to take his band to the French capital to boost the morale of troops on leave from the front lines. Miller and his band members were delighted with the proposal and readily accepted the offer.

Miller's executive officer (and personal manager during their civilian careers), Don Haynes, was dispatched to Paris to find accommodations for the band. While there he ran into Col. Norman F. Basselle, executive officer at the Milton Ernest Base in England. Miller had become friends with Colonel Basselle when his band appeared at the post. Basselle visited Paris often and had numerous contacts there. Moreover, he was anxious to do all he could to help the Miller band relocate to the Continent.

When Haynes got back to London, Miller and the band were just finishing a tiring set of recording sessions for their radio broadcasts, which would be played while they were in Europe. Haynes was scheduled to return to France on 14 December to finalize arrangements for the band's move and the AEF Christmas show, which was to be broadcast on Christmas day from the Olympia Theatre in Paris. Anxious to get things moving, Miller decided that he, rather than Haynes, would go to Paris.

Poor weather on the thirteenth canceled all flights. The following day Haynes met Colonel Basselle for lunch, and when the officer learned that Miller was going to Paris first instead of Haynes, he invited Miller to fly to Paris with him the next day in Brig. Gen. Donald R. Goodrich's private plane. Goodrich was assistant deputy commander for materiel for the European theater of operations. Miller accepted, but because the weather had not changed, he felt that there was little chance they would be leaving on the fifteenth. There had been no SHAEF shuttle to Paris for the past five days.

On 15 December, Basselle and Miller waited at Bedford for a call from the pilot, who was flying in from an air base some one hundred miles north to pick them up. The call finally came, and although it was cold, cloudy, and raining where Basselle and Miller waited, the pilot declared that the current weather forecast for the Continent was favorable. Basselle assured Miller that they would be safe because the pilot, Flight Officer John R. S. Morgan, was a veteran instrument aviator who had flown thirty-two missions in B-24s.

As they waited at nearby RAF Twinwoods Farm Air Field, the sound of an aircraft suddenly penetrated the gloom, and just before 1400 hours (2:00 P.M.) Morgan dropped from the overcast and landed his Canadian-built single-engine plane, a Noorduyn UC-64A Norseman. He taxied to where the two men stood and turned his craft into the wind on the runway while keeping the prop turning. Basselle and Miller loaded their gear aboard and then climbed in and took their seats. Basselle sat in the copilot's seat, and Miller sat behind him. With his passengers aboard, Morgan went to full throttle and released the brakes, and the aircraft gained speed as it roared down the runway. The plane was soon aloft, disappearing within minutes into the two-hundred-foot ceiling. That was the last anyone ever saw or heard of the aircraft and its passengers.

Ever since Glenn Miller disappeared, theories have abounded about what happened to him. The simplest and most probable explanation was that the flight was in trouble from the start, since the aircraft carried no deicing equipment. This meant that the plane had to remain under the heavy weather and fly just above the churning waves in the English Channel. General Goodrich apparently was furious when he learned that the plane had been used in those weather conditions. The aircraft may well have iced up and crashed into the sea. Some believe that the plane may have fallen victim to bombs jettisoned by a Royal Air Force squadron returning at that very time from an aborted air raid. A British navigator from that flight recalled seeing a small aircraft crash into the channel on the day Miller disappeared.

The Glenn Miller AAF Band continued to play for American and Allied soldiers in Europe under the able direction of longtime member Ray McKinley. In August 1945 the band arrived back in New York and a short time later made its final appearance, at the National Press Club in Washington, D.C. Among those attending were President Harry S. Truman, Gen. Dwight D. Eisenhower, and Gen. Hap Arnold. In a moving introduction, entertainer Eddie Cantor praised Glenn Miller's patriotism and the importance of the entire band to the morale of the Allied troops. Then, as the band broke into the strains of "Moonlight Serenade," President Truman rose and led the audience in a standing ovation. No other American musician or group had ever been so honored.

In February 1945, Helen Miller, wife of Glenn Miller for sixteen years, accepted the Bronze Star Medal awarded to her husband posthumously. The citation read:

For meritorious service in connection with military operations as Commander of the Army Air Forces Band (Special), from 9 July 1944 to 15 December 1944. Major Miller, through excellent judgment and professional skill, conspicuously blended the abilities of the outstanding musicians comprising the group into a harmonious orchestra whose noteworthy contribution to the morale of the armed forces has been little less than sensational. Major Miller constantly sought to increase the services rendered by his organization, and it was through him that the band was ordered to give this excellent entertainment to as many troops as possible. His superior accomplishments are highly commendable and reflect the highest credit upon himself and the armed forces of the United States.

Elvis Presley

The audience was restless with anticipation. It was an eclectic crowd at the arena that night, a kaleidoscope of ages, races, and nationalities, though predominantly female. They had come from nearby cities and neighboring states, and as far away as Europe and the Far East. They came for one reason only, and that reason had yet to appear. The opening acts—a comedian, a female gospel trio, an instrumental combo—had received dutiful but tepid applause. Intermission was interminable. But the crowd quieted with the announcement that the interval was concluding; the undercurrent of electricity swelled toward a fever pitch. The lights in the hall were extinguished and out of the blackness came the first strains of *Also Sprach Zarathustra*, more widely recognized as the theme from the movie *2001: A Space Odyssey*. As the music reached another crescendo and a thunder of drums brought the lights up, thousands of flashbulbs exploded in dizzying waves, and the screams of the fans reached a decibel level that shook the building. The King of Rock and Roll had taken the stage at last.

Elvis Aaron Presley was born in the sleepy town of Tupelo, Mississippi, on 8 January 1935 to Vernon Elvis and Gladys Smith Presley. His identical twin, Jesse Garon Presley, was stillborn. The senior Presley held a variety of jobs—cotton farmer, carpentry foreman, factory worker. Gladys was a devoted and protective mother. When Elvis turned ten he received his first guitar. What he really wanted was a .22 rifle, but Gladys had vetoed that idea as too expensive and too dangerous. She did, however, buy him the best guitar available; it cost $12.50.

Elvis learned some basic chords from his uncle, Vester Presley, and taught himself by singing and playing along with hillbilly tunes and African-American blues songs he heard on the radio.

The family attended services every Sunday at the First Assembly of God Church near their home in East Tupelo. Vernon Presley eventually became a deacon in the church. The preacher, Reverend Frank Smith, frequently played the guitar during his sermons. The power of the Holy Spirit was emphasized; music was permitted only to praise the Lord and, as long as the purpose was pure, any and all gyrations by the assembly were acceptable. Elvis gained his first singing experiences in the church choir and later at revivals and camp meetings.

The Presleys moved to Memphis, Tennessee, in 1949, when Elvis was just old enough to start high school. He attended L. C. Humes High, a technical and vocational school, and for the first two years the shy country boy went virtually unnoticed. Fellow students remembered him as a junior and senior only because of his flashy clothes and slick pompadour hair style, adopted in imitation of one of his favorite screen heroes, Tony Curtis. Upon graduating in 1953 Presley took a job as a truck driver for the Crown Electric Company. At night he studied to be an electrician.

Ever the thoughtful son, Elvis wanted a special gift for his mother's birthday that summer. The Sun Record Company in Memphis had a department that cut personal records, so he paid four dollars to make a recording of "My Happiness" and "That's When Your Heartaches Begin." Sam Phillips, president of Sun Records, heard the performance and was impressed enough to sign Presley to a contract. The next year Elvis made his first commercial recording for Sun, "That's All Right, Mama," backed with "Blue Moon of Kentucky." The first time Memphis disc jockey Dewey Phillips played the record on his radio program, *Red Hot and Blue,* the response was immediate: forty-seven phone calls and seventeen telegrams. By the next week, Memphis stores had sold more than six thousand copies of the record and Elvis Presley was on his way. Nevertheless, Presley kept his job with Crown Electric until several of his Sun recordings had been released and his agent was booking him for live appearances.

It was about that time that Presley made the acquaintance of impresario Thomas A. Parker, who had managed country music's "Tennessee Plowboy," Eddy Arnold, for several years. Although Arnold had had a recording contract with RCA at the time he met Parker, he was not yet a major star. Parker not only promoted Arnold's singing career but also got him a two-picture contract in Hollywood. Arnold, however, eventually became annoyed by "the Colonel's" overly aggressive management style and constant presence in his office, dressing room, and home, and he fired him in 1953. When Parker met Elvis in the summer of 1955, he was looking for an artist with a potential for national stardom; Elvis Presley seemed made to order.

Elvis had been managed by local disc jockey Bob Neal, who booked his performances. Neal's contract with Elvis ran until March 1956, but by the fall of 1955 Colonel Parker was already firmly in charge of Presley's career. Elvis undertook a personal appearance tour as the "Hillbilly Cat." Parker also signed him up to perform weekly on *Louisiana Hayride,* over station KWKH in Shreveport, Louisiana. Parker then engineered a buyout of Elvis's Sun Records contract by RCA Victor; Sun was paid thirty-five thousand dollars for the contract and five previously recorded master discs. Elvis received a bonus of five thousand dollars as part of the deal and promptly purchased a brand new pink-and-white Cadillac for his beloved mother, even though Gladys had no license and could not drive.

Presley's fame grew by leaps and bounds. RCA Victor pressed all five of Elvis's records under its own label. They were released simultaneously and within three months accounted for more than half of RCA's popular-music production. Television appearances followed, including *The Jackie Gleason Show, The Steve Allen Show, The Milton Berle Show,* and Tommy and Jimmy Dorsey's *Stage Show.*

When Parker negotiated a seven-year contract for Elvis with Hal Wallis Productions in 1956, a screen idol was born. The first of the thirty-three films Presley would eventually make was released in November 1956. *Love Me Tender,* like all of the Presley films, did not receive critical acclaim, but as with the others, it was a commercial success. *Loving You* followed in July 1957, and *Jailhouse Rock* four months later, for which Elvis earned $250,000 plus 50 percent of the net profits. His financial success enabled him to buy a new family home, a mansion called Graceland on thirteen acres at the edge of Memphis. Yet even his money and fame could not keep Uncle Sam from knocking on his door.

Elvis received his draft notice in December 1957 ordering him to report for duty in January. Because postponement of the scheduled filming of *King Creole* would present a severe corporate financial loss, Paramount Studios sent a letter to the draft board requesting a delay. The board, however, said such a request must come from Elvis himself, who sent it reluctantly; he wanted to get his required service behind him as quickly as possible. The delay was granted and Elvis reported to Fort Chaffee, Arkansas, on 24 March 1958.

No soldier was ever drafted into the Army with as much fanfare and publicity. More than fifty photographers and cameramen dogged his every step—the preinduction physical, the oath taking, the haircut, and the issuance of a uniform at the quartermasters. The world-famous singing sensation and movie star was now officially just Pvt. Elvis A. Presley, Serial No. 53310761.

After basic training and advanced instruction in tank corps operations at Fort Hood, Texas, Elvis was scheduled for duty with the 3d Armored Division in Friedberg, Germany, in September. While Elvis was on leave in Memphis in August, his mother, Gladys, who had been hospitalized for severe liver damage, suffered a heart attack and died. Elvis grieved deeply; he felt he was now truly alone in the world. His feelings for his mother were expressed in the inscription he selected for her tombstone: "Beloved wife of Vernon Presley and mother of Elvis Presley. She was the sunshine of our house." Elvis sent flowers to her grave once a week for as long as he lived.

Elvis Presley was inducted into the Army on 24 March 1958. After completing basic and advanced training, he was sent to Germany and assigned to the 1st Medium Tank Battalion, 32d Armor of the 3d Armored Division, located at Friedberg. Upon reporting for duty, he was assigned to a reconnaissance platoon. In February 1960 Sergeant Presley and a driver study a situation map before moving out while undergoing training at Grafenwohr, Germany. The following month Presley was honorably discharged and awarded a Good Conduct Medal. (National Archives)

Elvis's arrival in Germany drew a huge crowd of fans and a flurry of press coverage. But he soon settled into a routine. His father and grandmother arrived in October, and Presley rented a small house for the three of them in the nearby town of Bad Nauheim. Elvis resided there for the eighteen months he was in Germany, for the most part with a degree of anonymity, except for the sign in German someone posted outside the house that read "Autographs Between 7:00 and 8:00 PM Only."

Elvis was initially designated jeep driver for the commanding officer of Company D but was quickly transferred to Company C, a scout platoon, where he was assigned to drive for Reconnaissance Platoon Sgt. Ira Jones. C Company spent much of its time in the field on maneuvers, which helped remove Presley from the public eye.

Driving a jeep was a perfect assignment for Presley, who loved vehicles of any sort. He even enjoyed the work of jeep maintenance and, according to the recollection of a fellow soldier, "he was one of five who got a perfect rating after an inspection of over 300 vehicles." Another soldier remembered that Elvis would get down on his hands and knees and sandpaper the exhaust pipe to make it sparkle.

During his term of military service, Elvis requested no special treatment and performed all the basic duties of a soldier. His former commanding officer, Lt. William Taylor, Jr., described him as "a motivated and dedicated soldier." In March 1960 he was discharged at Fort Dix, New Jersey, as a sergeant with a Good Conduct Medal.

Elvis resumed his former lifestyle quickly, making television appearances and starting work on a new film, G.I. Blues, playing a soldier stationed in Germany who just happened to be able to sing. He still had legions of devoted fans, and his popularity remained high for several years, but the "British Invasion" of the mid-1960s, when the Beatles and other new talent from the British Isles hit the American music scene, pushed Presley and his music into the background.

The idol of millions of women married Priscilla Beaulieu on 1 May 1967 in a secret ceremony at a Las Vegas hotel. Priscilla had been a fourteen-year-old Army brat when she met Presley in 1959 in Germany, where her father was stationed. Their relationship blossomed over the ensuing years, and she even lived at Graceland, with the approval of her parents, while she finished high school. Their daughter, Lisa Marie Presley, was born exactly nine months after the wedding.

In the early 1970s Elvis resumed concert and nightclub work with amazing success. His fans now numbered the children of parents who themselves had remained ardent followers for nearly two decades. Honors and awards still came his way, and in 1972 Memphis renamed the road that passed in front of Graceland, Elvis Presley Boulevard. He also continued to accumulate gold records (sales of one million copies) until his death. At the end of the twentieth century Elvis was still the preeminent singer in terms of gold records achieved: sixty-two. Barbra Streisand was a distant second at forty, followed by the Beatles with thirty-nine.

Although he continued to perform, the pressures of Elvis's lifestyle and the toll of his divorce from Priscilla in 1973 led to the star's deteriorating health. His junk-food diet and significant weight gain contributed as well. Presley's sudden death of a heart attack in 1977 at the age of forty-two shocked the world. Following a private funeral, Elvis was laid to rest next to his mother on the grounds of Graceland, in an area that Elvis had called the Meditation Garden. Priscilla Presley subsequently opened Graceland to the public, and to this day thousands of Presley fans tour the home and pass by his grave, placing flowers and other tributes on it. A large commemoration occurs each year on 16 August, the anniversary of his death.

Elvis Presley's influence on American popular music and lifestyle was considerable. Critics may say he was not the greatest entertainer of all time. His millions of fans, however, would take exception to that; to them, he was, is, and always will be the King of Rock and Roll.

Ronald Reagan

R onald Reagan is to date the only movie actor to ascend to the presidency of the United States. Prior to his film career he was a sportscaster for a Des Moines, Iowa, radio station, whose duties included announcing Chicago Cubs games from Morse code transmissions. In the mid-1930s Reagan traveled to Hollywood. After signing with Warner Brothers, he was cast in some fifty movies, mainly B productions. Among the more notable films in which he appeared were *Knute Rockne—All American* (1940), *Santa Fe Trail* (1940), and *King's Row* (1942).

Several years after graduating from Eureka College in Illinois and while employed by station WHO in Des Moines, he started taking home-study U.S. Army extension courses. Upon completing a number

(U.S. Government Printing Office)

of them, he joined the Army's enlisted reserve corps at Des Moines in 1937 as a private in Troop B, 322d Cavalry. In May of the same year he was appointed a second lieutenant in the officers' reserve corps of the cavalry and the following month accepted an officer's commission.

In the spring of 1937 Reagan followed the Chicago Cubs to southern California for spring training. He had long harbored an interest in acting and decided to go for a screen test while he was in such close proximity to Hollywood. Shortly after he returned to Des Moines he received a telegram with the offer of a contract from Warner Brothers. He said his good byes, packed up his newly purchased Nash convertible, and in June arrived at the gates of the studio lot in Burbank. Reagan acted in numerous movies over the next four years and achieved some critical success as "the Gipper" in the 1940 film about legendary Notre Dame football coach Knute Rockne.

Ronald Reagan was still an Army Reserve officer, and when the Japanese bombed Pearl Harbor, he knew that he would be called up. Initially he was ordered to report to Fort Mason, the port of embarkation in San Francisco. He was assigned as liaison officer loading convoys with troops bound for Australia because he was discovered to have vision problems and was "confined to the continental limits, eligible for corps area service command or War Department overhead only." The assignment lasted about three months, when he was transferred to Army Air Force Intelligence in Los Angeles.

At that time Gen. Hap Arnold was building a giant bomber fleet to fly combat missions in Europe. Arnold had established the intelligence unit to make training films and documentaries and to train camera crews. Reagan was ordered to the unit because of his experience in motion pictures. He was responsible for recruiting from various studios for the unit, gathering film industry personnel who were ineligible for the draft. Reagan also had first call on draftees with film experience.

The group took over the Hal Roach Studios in Culver City. Known officially as the First Motion Picture Unit, it was nicknamed "Fort Roach." Reagan was initially assigned as unit adjutant and personnel officer. The training films subsequently produced by this talent-laden group found their way to U.S. fighting units around the world. It could be said that the First Motion Picture Unit served as the Signal Corps for General Arnold's new Air Force.

One of the unit's most significant achievements was the development of a new briefing procedure for pilots and bombardiers. Under the old method, an intelligence officer would brief the fliers before a mission from a map marked with target sites and entry and exit routes for the aircraft. But by using prewar photographs and intelligence reports, Reagan's intelligence unit made the entire floor of a sound stage into a photo mosaic of the target area. A camera mounted on a moveable overhead derrick was run across the floor, providing a near-movie

Popular film star Ronald Reagan was in the Army Reserve when America entered World War II. Poor eyesight kept him out of combat, but his entertainment background proved invaluable to AAF training operations. He was assigned to the AAF's First Motion Picture Unit, located at the old Hal Roach Studios in Culver City, California. Often referred to as Culver City Cowboys, members of the unit made sophisticated training and propaganda films using the talents of artists and filmmakers in uniform. Captain Reagan narrated many of the films. Honorably discharged in December 1945, Reagan eventually served as commander in chief when he was elected the nation's fortieth president (1981–89). Shown is Captain Reagan at work during World War II. (U.S. Air Force)

replica of the target. The picture was updated periodically from bomb-damage assessment photography so that mission briefings were kept current. These films were dispatched to the operating forces as quickly as possible. They were particularly effective during the bombing campaign against the Japanese home islands. Reagan narrated the films, taking crewmen through a detailed briefing of check points and terrain features along the way and, once over the target area, calling out, "Bombs away."

While at Fort Roach, Reagan was privy to classified photography of the German concentration camps and the horrors of nazism. The images of the pitiful inmates who survived the camps became forever etched in his mind.

Lieutenant Reagan was promoted to first lieutenant on 14 January 1943. The following month he was ordered to the Provisional Task Force Show Unit for the filming of *This Is the Army,* a show put together by Irving Berlin to benefit Army Relief, in which Reagan was cast in a starring role. He returned to the First Motion Picture Unit after this duty and was promoted to captain on 22 July 1943.

In January 1944 Reagan was ordered on temporary duty to New York City to participate in the opening of the fourth War Loan Drive. He was personally singled out for the job by the secretary of the treasury in a letter to the secretary of war. When the assignment was over, Reagan again returned to the motion picture unit. In November 1944 he was assigned to the 18th AAF Base Unit at Culver City, where he remained until the end of the war. In 1945 Reagan was recommended for promotion to major, but there was no major's vacancy in his unit at that time and the request was not approved. On 9 December 1945 he was honorably discharged from the AAF. His commission in the Officer's Reserve Corp was terminated by law on 1 April 1953.

While with the First Motion Picture Unit and the 18th AAF Base Unit, Ronald Reagan served in various capacities. He was at one time or another personnel officer, post adjutant, executive officer, and commanding officer. By the end of the war his military units had produced some four hundred training films for the Army Air Forces.

Following his departure from the service, Reagan returned to Hollywood and appeared in movies up until the 1960s. His last film was *The Killers* (1964). He became increasingly involved in the business aspect of the industry over time, and he served as president of the Screen Actors Guild from 1947 to 1952 and in 1959. Reagan had gained a reputation as a staunch liberal, but in 1962 he professed a change to conservatism, and in 1964 he strongly supported Barry Goldwater's presidential campaign. He survived Goldwater's defeat to run and become elected as governor of California in 1966, the first Republican to hold that office in many years.

Reagan served eight years in California's top job, and during that time he became an influential force in the Republican Party. Nevertheless, he lost his bid for the GOP nomination for the presidency to incumbent Gerald Ford in 1976. Four years later, however, he was elected president of the United States. President Reagan served for two terms, and among numerous accomplishments, he is credited by many with ending the cold war.

Ronald Reagan married actress Jane Wyman, a colleague at Warner Brothers, before the war. They had two children, Maureen and Michael, but the marriage was dissolved in 1948. Today, he and his second wife, Nancy (former actress Nancy Davis), live in quiet retirement in California.

Young Dutch Reagan

Household discussions of Ronald Reagan's early days in Iowa are recalled by coauthor Paul Wilderson from the 1950s, when his family gathered around the small screen on Sunday evenings to watch *General Electric Theater,* a show long hosted by the actor. Wilderson's father, Paul Wilderson, Jr., who was born and grew up in Des Moines, was a senior in high school in 1936. At the Standard gas station where he worked after school, he was regularly assigned to grease and wash the local announcer's brown Nash coupe. The service station was only a few blocks from radio station WHO, and it was an easy walk for Reagan, who would drop the car off on his way to work. The coauthor's mother, Helen Wilderson, remembered that Dutch Reagan, as he then was known, was a regular announcer at the Roosevelt High School football games on Friday nights, and that the local girls would strain to get a glimpse of the handsome sportscaster as he walked by in his felt hat and camel-hair jacket. It is clear that Ronald Reagan was already something of a celebrity and was making an impression.

Mickey Rooney

For moviegoers of the late 1930s and the 1940s, musicals abounded. It was a time when audiences became enraptured with the singing and dancing talents of a generation of artists rarely seen before or after. Among the most popular movies of the time were the Andy Hardy films, sentimental comedies that focused on the goodness of domestic tranquility and the simple life. Andy Hardy was played by Mickey Rooney, a five-foot, three-inch bundle of energy and talent who, in addition to being a fine actor, could sing, dance, play the drums, mimic other actors, and tell jokes. His sidekick in a number of these films was singer Judy Garland, who went on to play Dorothy in the classic film *The Wizard of Oz* and become a legendary talent in her own right.

The Hardy films almost always included a "barnyard show." One of the characters would say, "Let's do a show!" and a frantic energy would overtake the cast until they came up with a musical production worthy of the best shows offered on Broadway. *Babes in Arms* (1939) was typical of the Andy Hardy movies, featuring enthusiastic players marching through their idyllic town singing the film's theme song, ready to "do a show." It was rousing good fun for both the actors and the audience.

Mickey Rooney was born Joe Yule, Jr., on 23 September 1920, the son of vaudeville performers. He made his first stage appearance at the age of fifteen months and his movie debut at six years in the silent film *Not to be Trusted* (1926). During the next six years he starred in fifty comedies in the Mickey McGuire series, in which he played a popular comic strip character. Yule changed his name to Mickey McGuire and shortly thereafter, as he began to be cast in feature films at Universal Studios and other movie companies, he changed it again to Mickey Rooney.

In 1937 Rooney appeared in the first of fifteen Andy Hardy films. The popular series made him a household name, and his fortunes continued to climb with his appearance in *Boy's Town* (1938), which starred Spencer Tracy as Father Flanagan. He teamed up with Judy Garland in several subsequent musicals. In 1938 he was awarded a special Academy Award for "significant contribution in bringing to the screen the spirit and personification of youth, and as a juvenile player setting a high standard of ability and achievement."

Rooney became the top movie box-office draw in the early 1940s when he was featured in *The Human Comedy* (1943) and *National Velvet* (1944). His career, however, was interrupted by his Army service during World War II. Initially classified 4-F because of high blood pressure, he again visited the Selective Service Center and asked for new tests. He passed the second time and was reclassified 1-A. *National Velvet* was in production at the time, and MGM decided to shoot Rooney's scenes first when he was told that he would be called up for Army service within a month. His costar in the movie was twelve-year-old Elizabeth Taylor.

In June 1944 Mickey Rooney was inducted into the Army at Fort MacArthur, near San Pedro, California. Three days later he was on a troop train headed for cavalry training at Fort Riley, Kansas. He enjoyed the forced marches, the heavy packs, the obstacle courses, and the hours he spent on the rifle range. He qualified for the sharpshooter badge with an automatic rifle. Within two weeks the actor was made a squad leader. One of the men in the squad took exception to Rooney's selection as leader, saying that he only got the position because he was a movie star. Rooney would not stand for such guff, and the two had it out in a fierce bare-knuckle fight with the entire squad watching until it was finally broken up. Afterward, the two men bought each other a beer; the incident ended any thoughts by others about taking Rooney on.

In September Rooney was sent to Camp Sibert, Alabama, for training in chemical warfare. Before he could start, however, he was assigned to the 6817th Special Services Battalion. It appeared that USO entertainers did not want any part of performing on the front lines, so the Army decided to use their own men to do the job and scoured units for actors, comedians, musicians, and singers. Rooney soon was headed for an Army base near New York to make ready for going overseas. Although the 6817th sailed on the luxurious *Queen Mary* for England, the trip was no picnic. The Army managed to cram some seven thousand soldiers onto the ship, which was built to accommodate about one thousand passengers. The group ended up at the Tenth Replacement Center in Lichfield, a small town near Birmingham, England. Besides putting on shows nightly at Lichfield, the entertainers were ordered to spend twenty-one days of KP duty just to prove that they were not being given special treatment.

When Rooney and the troops arrived in France, the Army had an immediate problem. The combat forces were moving so fast at the front that the logistics involved in moving 153 entertainers together around Western Europe was deemed impossible. The solution agreed upon by higher authority was to split the group into three-man teams, give them a jeep, and send them off across the European theater. Rooney came forward with the idea for the teams to perform in barns, which proved to work for many of their shows. The jeep shows consisted of a musician, a singer, and an MC who told jokes. They carried additional musical instruments with them to vary each program. Rooney acted as the MC on his team, which gave its first show three miles from the front between two Sherman tanks in a Belgian snowstorm. Their audience consisted of some sixty combat troopers who applauded the performance enthusiastically.

Mickey Rooney was inducted into the Army in June 1944 and after completing basic training was assigned to the 6817th Special Services Battalion. He served in France as part of the "jeep show" operation: three entertainers were assigned a jeep and speaker equipment and sent out to perform shows for front-line troops. They often found themselves in the middle of combat situations, as did Rooney and his companions. Honorably discharged in March 1946, Staff Sergeant Rooney was awarded a Bronze Star and a Good Conduct Medal. Here Rooney signs autographs for British troops in Belgium. (Photofest)

The jeep show teams lived mostly on C rations and often would go for weeks without shaving or bathing. In early 1945 Rooney's small troupe visited a headquarters company near Radonge, Belgium, in weather that was fiercely cold. They introduced themselves to the officer-in-charge and offered to put on a show. Enthusiastically received by the officer, Rooney and his men retrieved their gear from the jeep, but as they entered the headquarters a general burst into the room. He eyed Rooney and asked what was going on. When Rooney informed him that they were about to put on a show, the general replied that they were welcome to stay and perform but he had just ordered the headquarters to be blown up in eight minutes and for their own good they had better "haul ass" as fast as they could.

Rooney and his team jumped in their jeep and raced down the road from the headquarters as fast as the vehicle would take them. They moved so fast, in fact, that they soon found themselves lost. Hearing an unfamiliar sound, they stopped the jeep and quickly realized that it must be a tank. Five hundred yards ahead they spotted the tank moving through the brush. They could plainly see a swastika on its side and an 88-millimeter cannon protruding from the turret. Lost or not, they pulled back onto the road and just kept moving.

Rooney's group did many shows near the front lines and multiple shows on a single day, sometimes running into the early morning hours. On one such occasion they finished at 3:15 A.M. and about an hour later their audience left to fight the battle of Remagen to reach German soil. Several hours after that Rooney saw many of the same soldiers coming back on stretchers, some of them dead. It was at Remagen that the Americans by accident found an intact railway bridge that the Germans had failed to destroy. Though the Germans pounded it mercilessly, U.S. troops poured across it until it finally collapsed. More than one hundred engineers were on the bridge when it fell; twenty-eight of them died. By then, pontoon bridges had gone up nearby and Allied troops continued to cross into the heart of Germany.

Rooney and his group played many hospitals and saw much of the carnage caused by war. The actor still vividly remembers visiting MASH units in which ten operating tables were occupied at once. There was not much he could do but go from bed to bed and talk to the wounded. On one occasion he comforted a young soldier who showed Rooney a picture of his girl back home. The soldier was deeply distressed because he was going to lose a leg in the morning. He wondered if she would have him when he returned home as an amputee. Rooney consoled him with the story of English actor Herbert Marshall, who lost a leg in World War I and yet became a brilliant actor. Rooney promised the soldier that his girlfriend would be waiting for him when he got back.

Years later when Rooney was having a drink at the Fairmont Hotel in San Francisco, a man beckoned him to his table. He did not recognize the man, but it turned out to be the young soldier he had consoled during the war. His girl had indeed been there when he returned home. They married, had three children, and by that time he was an executive at Boeing. "You helped me come back, Rooney, at a time in my life when I needed help," the former soldier toasted the actor. "Here's to you. You're a helluva guy. Thank you." They touched glasses and Rooney answered, "And so are you, you're a helluva guy too."

Rooney's group continued their entertainment duty, following various divisions of the 12th Army Group and the 83d Airborne, as well as Patton's Third Army Division. They covered more than 150,000 miles during the first year. Rooney was one of the first Americans to visit the concentration camp at Dachau, where he was horrified by what he saw and astonished at what one group of human beings could inflict upon another.

After the shooting war ended on 7 May 1945, the jeep shows wound down and the entertainers gradually got back together to put on larger, more extravagant productions. In September Rooney directed an original musical review called *O.K.-USA* in Mannheim, Germany. His last duty in Europe was with the Armed Forces Radio Network, where he served as an announcer and entertainer. Finally, with enough points accumulated to return home, he found his way to Le Havre and boarded the *General G. O. Squire* for New York.

Rooney was offered a commission before he departed, but he turned it down. He had seen enough of war during his one year, eight months, and twenty-one days in the Army, and he was anxious to return to his wife, Betty Jane, his son, and his former life. Rooney had made sergeant by the time he was discharged from the service. He had earned the Bronze Star Medal, a Good Conduct Medal, the European–African–Middle Eastern Campaign Medal with seven bronze star devices, the World War II Victory Medal, and a sharpshooter badge with an automatic rifle bar.

Upon returning to Hollywood, Rooney found little work, and his career went into a decline. In 1948 he severed his ties with MGM and formed his own production company. It failed, and he found himself in financial trouble, a pattern that would continue over the years. Each time Rooney seemed to be down and out, he would bounce back with the same old determination and enthusiasm he had displayed in his younger days. Financial problems continued to plague him, however, in large part because of alimony payments he was forced to make to eight former wives, the first of whom had been actress Ava Gardner.

Rooney developed into a fine character actor in films such as *The Bold and the Brave* (1956) and *Baby Face Nelson* (1957). During the 1960s and 1970s he continued to appear in movies, on television, and in nightclubs. In 1978 Rooney announced his retirement. A year later, however, he made a sensational Broadway debut in the musical *Sugar Babies* and later toured with the road company of the hit show. He was nominated for a best supporting actor Academy Award in 1979 for *The Black Stallion*. In 1982 he was awarded an Emmy for his performance in the television movie *Bill,* and that same year he received an honorary Oscar "in recognition of his 60 years of versatility in a variety of memorable performances." Seemingly unable to quit working, Rooney in 1993 joined the cast of Broadway's *Will Rogers Follies*. The masterful entertainer has appeared in more than 140 films. Mickey Rooney remains active today in the theater and the film industry, as well as in numerous business ventures.

PART 3

Others Who Served

Others Who Served

This book is not, of course, all-inclusive. Many other actors wore khaki during World War I, World War II, the Korean War, and afterward. Here are a few of them. Their most notable film and television appearances appear in parentheses.

Abbott, Art
Served as B-17 pilot in the Army Air Force during World War II. (Films: *Sweet Bird of Youth*/1962.)

Alda, Alan
Joined the Army Reserve after graduating from Fordham University. Did six-month tour as gunnery officer (rank of captain) during Korean War and gained invaluable experience for his later career.

(Films: *Crimes and Misdemeanors*/1989, *Whispers in the Dark*/1992; TV: best remembered as Hawkeye Pierce in the Emmy Award–winning series *M*A*S*H*/1972–83.)

Allen, Steve

Drafted in 1943, he served for only five months and received medical discharge for asthma. (Films: *The Benny Goodman Story*/1956, *The Sunshine Boys*/1975; TV: starred in popular *Steve Allen Show* in the 1950s.) Allen also has written numerous popular songs, including the ballad "It's Impossible," recorded by Perry Como.

Andes, Keith

Enlisted in the Army Air Force in 1942. Went in as cadet and came out an actor. Assigned to Special Services; performed in Army Air Force musical *Winged Victory*. Signed by David Selznick with understanding that his contract would become effective when he was discharged. (Films: *Tora, Tora, Tora*/1970, in which he played Gen. George C. Marshall.)

Arnaz, Desi

Drafted into the Army in May 1942. Injured knee during basic training and classified for limited duty. Ordered to special Army training camp, where he taught illiterate draftees reading and writing. Transferred to Birmingham Hospital, Van Nuys, California, where he eased the suffering of wounded and mentally disturbed combat veterans by providing entertainment. His wife, film star Lucille Ball, assisted his efforts by convincing movie executives to provide starlets to hand out refreshments to patients and serve as dancing partners. Honorably discharged in 1945. (Films: *Four Jacks and a Jill*/1942, *Bataan*/1943; TV: costarred with his wife in series *I Love Lucy*/1951–57.)

Arness, James

Drafted in February 1943 and completed basic training at Camp Wheeler, Georgia. Sent to North Africa, then Naples, Italy. Assigned to the 7th Regiment of the 3d Infantry Division. Wounded at Anzio and medically discharged at Camp Carson, Colorado, in January 1945.

Awarded the Bronze Star Medal, the Purple Heart Medal, the Good Conduct Medal, and the European-Mideast Campaign Medal. Coauthor James Wise is currently working with Mr. Arness to write the star's biography. (Films: *Battleground*/1949, *The Thing*/1951; TV: starred as Marshall Matt Dillon on the Emmy Award–winning *Gunsmoke*/1955–75, which holds the record for the longest running television series.)

Asner, Ed

Drafted in July 1951 and trained as a radarman. Sent to France, where he managed a highly rated unit basketball team. (Films: *Fort Apache the Bronx*/1981, *JFK*/1991; TV: starred in comedy series *The Mary Tyler Moore Show*/1970–77, *Lou Grant*/1977–82.)

Bartholomew, Freddie

Served during World War II as an Army Air Force maintenance crewman. (Films: *Little Lord Fauntleroy*/1936, *The Swiss Family Robinson*/1940.)

Bean, Orson

Enlisted in 1946 for eighteen-month tour. Sent to Fort Knox, Kentucky, for basic training. Sailed for Yokohama, Japan, in December 1946 for occupation duty. Assigned to 81st Airborne Artillery in Koi Zumi, Japan, fifty miles north of Tokyo. Lived in a converted aircraft factory learning how to operate howitzers and pulling guard duty. On days off he traveled to Tokyo, where he witnessed the devastation the city had suffered from firebombing during the closing months of World War II. Honorably discharged in 1948. (TV: comedian Bean cohosted *The Blue Angel* variety series with Polly Bergen/1954, appeared in *Fernwood*/1977–78, served as frequent game-show panelist on *To Tell the Truth*/1956–66 and *Laugh Line*/1959, and occasional guest host on Jack Paar's *Tonight Show*/1960–62.)

Best, James

Served one and a half years as a military policeman attached to the Ninth Army Air Force during World War II. Credited with capturing two wanted Nazi war criminals, he was awarded a citation for his action. (Films: *The Naked and the Dead*/1958, *Sounder*/1972.)

Bishop, Joey

Drafted in 1942 and served as recreational director at Fort Sam Houston, Texas. (Films: *Ocean's Eleven*/1960, *Valley of the Dolls*/1967.) Comedian was a member of Frank Sinatra's "Rat Pack" in the 1960s, which also included Sammy Davis, Jr., Peter Lawford, and Dean Martin.

Blocker, Dan

Drafted in 1950 and sent to Korea, where he was assigned to the 45th Infantry Division. Discharged in 1953 with the rank of sergeant. Museum established in his honor in O'Donnell, Texas. (Films: *Come Blow Your Horn*/1963, *The Cockeyed Cowboys of Calico County*/ 1969; TV: played Hoss in the popular western series *Bonanza*/1959–72.)

Boles, John

Served in World War I and was involved in espionage activities in Germany, Bulgaria, and Turkey. Appeared in numerous movies between 1924 and 1952. (Films: *Stella Dallas*/1937, *Thousands Cheer*/1943.)

Brady, Pat

Served with General Patton's Third Army during World War II. Was awarded two Purple Heart Medals for wounds received in France. (Films: *West of Cheyenne*/1938, *The Durango Kid*/1940, *Song of Texas*/1943; TV: *The Roy Rogers Show*/1951–57; originally sang with western group, Sons of the Pioneers, replacing Leonard Slye, a.k.a. Roy Rogers, when Rogers left the group to become a movie actor.)

Brennan, Walter

Spent nineteen months (1917–19) in France with American Expeditionary Force in 101st Field Artillery. He engaged in combat and also entertained in camp shows. (Films: *My Darling Clementine*/1946, *Red River*/1948, *Bad Day at Black Rock*/1955; TV: *The Real McCoys*/ 1957–62, television's first successful rural sitcom, and *The Guns of*

Will Sonnett/1968–69. First actor to win three Academy Awards as best supporting actor; appeared in more than one hundred films.)

Bronson, Charles

Drafted in late 1942. Served three years in the Army Air Force. As a private first class he was assigned to the 760th Mess Squadron in Kingman, Arizona. Hollywood biographies and press releases state that after his Arizona tour he was attached to a B-29 Superfortress squadron in the Pacific, where he completed twenty-five missions as a gunner and received a Purple Heart Medal for wounds received in combat. The data could not be confirmed because his service records were destroyed in a fire at the St. Louis National Personnel Records Center in 1973. (Films: *The Magnificent Seven*/1960, *The Dirty Dozen*/1967, *Death Wish*/1974; TV: *Man with a Camera*/1958–60, *The Travels of Jamie McPheeters*/1963–64, *Raid on Entebbe*/1977.)

Brooks, Mel

Enlisted in July 1944. Trained as a combat engineer and ordered to Europe to deactivate enemy mines. Eventually appeared in Army entertainment reviews. Honorably discharged in 1947. (Films: *Blazing Saddles*/1973, *Silent Movie*/1976, *High Anxiety*/1977, *History of the World—Part I*/1981, *To Be or Not To Be*/1985, *Spaceballs*/1987, *Robin Hood: Men in Tights*/1993.)

Burton, Robert

Served in World War I with the Wildcat Division (engineers). Spent eighteen months in France and discharged as a top sergeant. (Films: *Spirit of St. Louis*/1957, *Birdman of Alcatraz*/1962.)

Buttons, Red

Inducted in 1943. Performed in Army Air Force musical *Winged Victory*. One of service entertainers who performed at the Potsdam Conference outside Berlin in August 1945. Discharged with rank of corporal in 1946. (Films: *Sayonara*/1957, *The Poseidon Adventure*/1972, *It Could Happen to You*/1994; TV: *The Red Buttons Show*/1952.)

Cabot, Bruce

Served in Army Air Force during World War II as an intelligence officer in North Africa, Sicily, and Italy. (Films: *Cat Ballou*/1965, *The Green Berets*/1968.)

Carroll, John

Served in the Army Air Force during World War II in North Africa. Survived air crash that broke his back. (Films: *The Farmer Takes a Wife*/1953, *The Flying Tigers*/1956.)

Chandler, Jeff

Served four years in the Aleutians during World War II. (Films: *Broken Arrow*/1950, *The Battle at Apache Pass*/1952, *Away All Boats*/1956, *Merrill's Marauders*/1962.) Star of western and action movies died prematurely from blood poisoning in 1961.

Cobb, Lee J.

Enlisted in Army Air Force at age thirty-two. Attached to radio production unit in California for duration of war. Appeared in AAF musical *Winged Victory*. (Films: *Captain from Castile*/1947, *The Man in the Gray Flannel Suit*/1956, *Twelve Angry Men*/1957, *Exodus*/1960, *How the West Was Won*/1966, *The Exorcist*/1973.)

Coburn, James

Served as radio operator during World War II. (Films: *The Magnificent Seven*/1960, *Charade*/1963, *The Great Escape*/1963, *Our Man Flint*/1966, *Pat Garrett and Billy the Kid*/1973, *Hudson Hawk*/1991. Won Oscar for best supporting actor in 1999 for *Affliction*.)

Colleano, Bonar

Enlisted in Army Air Force during World War II. Injury forced him from active duty and he was transferred to Special Services to perform in camp shows. (Films: *Eight Iron Men*/1952, *Interpol*/1957.)

Conway, Tim

Served two years as a private during Korean War; stationed in Seattle. (Films: *McHale's Navy*/1964, *The Apple Dumpling Gang*/1975, *The Prize Fighter*/1979; TV: *McHale's Navy*/1962–66, *Rango*/1967, *The Carol Burnett Show*/1967–78, *The Tim Conway Show*/1970, 1980–81.)

Cook, Elisha, Jr.

Served in the Army Air Force during World War II. Stationed at Will Rogers Field in Oklahoma and appeared in numerous training films. (Films: *The Maltese Falcon*/1941, *Dillinger*/1944, *Rosemary's Baby*/1968.)

Cox, Wally

Drafted in 1942. Suffered heat stroke during basic training and medically discharged after four months in service. (Films: *State Fair*/1962, *The Bedford Incident*/1965; TV: *Mister Peepers*/1952–55, *The Adventures of Hiram Holliday*/1956–57. The voice of *Underdog*, a durable weekend cartoon series/1964–70, 1972–73.)

Crawford, Broderick

Served as sergeant in Army Air Force, 1942–45. (Films: *Born Yesterday*/1950, *War's Moon*/1981; TV: starred in series *Highway Patrol*/1955–59, *King of Diamonds*/1961, *The Interns*/1970–71.)

Cummings, Robert

Godson of Orville Wright, he served as flight instructor during World War II. (Films: *Wells Fargo*/1937, *The Devil and Miss Jones*/1941, *Kings Row*/1942, *Dial M for Murder*/1954, *What a Way to Go!*/1964; TV: starred in *Love That Bob*/1955–59, *The Bob Cummings Show*/1961–62.)

Daly, James

Served in Army and Navy during World War II. (Films: *The Court-Martial of Billy Mitchell*/1955, *Planet of the Apes*/1968; TV: *Medical Center* 1969–76.) Father of actors Tyne Daly (star of TV series *Cagney and Lacey*/1982–88, *Judging Amy*/1999–) and Tim Daly (*Wings*/1990–94).

Damone, Vic

An established TV, nightclub, and recording star, he was inducted in May 1951 for two-year hitch. Assigned to Special Services in Germany and given job as costume sorter. While on leave met Italian actress Pier Angeli, making a movie in Munich at the time. They subsequently married in 1954. (Films: *Kismet*/1955, *Spree*/1967; TV: *The Vic Damone Show*/1956–57, 1967; hosted a half-hour musical variety show, *The Lively Ones*/1962–63.)

Davis, Ossie

Inducted in 1942 and served in Liberia, West Africa, as a surgical technician. Discharged in 1945. (Films: *No Way Out*/1950, *The Joe Louis Story*/1953, *The Scalphunters*/1968, *Do the Right Thing*/1989, *Joe versus the Volcano*/1990, *Malcolm X*/1992; TV: *Ossie and Ruby!* [with wife, Ruby Dee]/1980–81, *Evening Shade*/1990–94.)

Derek, John

Enlisted in 1944 and volunteered for paratrooper training. Made sixteen jumps before discharge in 1946. (Films: *I'll Be Seeing You*/1945, *All the King's Men*/1949, *An Annapolis Story*/1955, *The Ten Commandments*/1956, *Exodus*/1960, *Bolero*/1984; TV: *Frontier Circus*/1961–62.) Disappointed in acting career, he became a proficient still photographer and later a movie cameraman and director. Married at various times to Ursula Andress, Linda Evans, and Bo Derek.

Dexter, Brad

Served four years during World War II, two of them touring the nation in Army Air Force musical *Winged Victory*. (Films: *The Asphalt Jungle*/1950, *Von Ryan's Express*/1965, *Shampoo*/1975.)

Donlevy, Brian

Hollywood press releases and media interviews state he was a fourteen-year-old bugler for General Pershing in the 1916 Mexican campaign against Pancho Villa, and that he flew with the Lafayette Esca-drille in World War I. None of the above information could be con-firmed. Official records do show that he spent two years at the U.S. Naval Academy as part of the class of 1921. (Films: *Beau Geste*/1939, *The Great McGinty*/1940, *Wake Island*/1942, *Two Years Before the Mast*/1946, *The Big Combo*/1955, *The Curse of the Fly*/1965; TV: *Dangerous Assignment*/1952, a half-hour adventure series the actor originated on radio in 1940.)

Duvall, Robert
Drafted in 1953. Spent tour of duty in the Signal Corps at Camp Gor-don near Augusta, Georgia. (Films: *The Godfather*/1972, *Network*/1976, *Apocalypse Now*/1979, *The Great Santini*/1980, *The Natural*/1984, *Days of Thunder*/1990, *Geronimo*/1993, *The Scarlet Letter*/1995.)

Farr, Jamie
Served as radio writer and producer for Armed Forces Radio Ser-vice during the Korean War. (Films: *With Six You Get Eggroll*/1968, *The Cannonball Run*/1981; TV: starred in *M*A*S*H*/1972–83.)

Fisher, Eddie
Inducted for two-year tour in 1951. Assigned to the U.S. Army Band and recruiting duty. Headlined the service's Armed Forces Review and gave more than 150 singing performances at bases in Pacific and Eu-rope. (Films: *Butterfield 8*/1960, *Nothing Lasts Forever*/1984; TV: *Coke Time*/1953–57, *The Eddie Fisher Show*/1957–59.)

Forrest, Steve
Staff sergeant/radio operator during World War II. Suffered frozen feet during Battle of the Bulge in December 1944 and hospitalized. (Films: *North Dallas Forty*/1979, *Sahara*/1984.) Brother of late actor Dana Andrews.

Franz, Arthur
Served in Army Air Force in Europe during World War II as a gun-ner and a navigator and was shot down twice. On one occasion he was

the lone survivor of his crew. Captured and imprisoned but rescued by an underground unit and taken to safety and hospitalization in Italy. (Films: *The Caine Mutiny*/1954, *That Championship Season*/1982.)

Gobel, George

Enlisted in the Army Air Force in 1943. Pilot and flight instructor in B-26 Marauders. Spent entire World War II service in Oklahoma and honorably discharged as first lieutenant in 1945. Often heard to say, "Not one Japanese plane got past Tulsa." (Films: *The Birds and the Bees*/1956, *I Married a Woman*/1957; TV: star of *The George Gobel Show*/1954–60. Awarded an Emmy in 1954.)

Gordon, Leo

Served in the Army Air Force for two years during World War II. (Films: *Tobruk*/1966, *Maverick*/1994.)

Graves, Peter

Served in the Army Air Force as a maintenance air crewman for two years during World War II. (Films: *Stalag 17*/1953, *The Long Gray Line*/1955, *The Court-Martial of Billy Mitchell*/1955, *Texas Across the River*/1966, *Cruise Missile*/1977, *Airplane!*/1980, *Savannah Smiles*/1982; TV: *Fury*/1955–66, *Mission Impossible*/1966–72.) Brother of actor James Arness of *Gunsmoke* fame.

Hackett, Buddy

Served three years with antiaircraft unit. On furlough in 1945 he saw Broadway production of *Oklahoma* and found his calling. (Films: *The Music Man*/1962, *It's a Mad, Mad, Mad, Mad World*/1963; TV: star of half-hour sitcom *Stanley*/1956–57, frequent guest on talk shows and game shows over the years.)

Heflin, Van

Enlisted in 1942 and later commissioned as second lieutenant. Assigned to 53d Field Artillery at Camp Roberts in California, where he trained cannoneers. Prior to overseas posting was denied combat duty because of old back injury but approved for limited duty. Requested transfer to Army Air Force as a 16-mm camera combat photographer and assigned to Medium Bombardment Division of Ninth Air Force in Europe. Involved in both air operations and ground assignments. Honorably discharged in 1945. (Films: *Annapolis Salute*/1937, *Santa Fe Trail*/1940, *Johnny Eager* [won Oscar for best supporting actor]/1942, *Green Dolphin Street*/1947, *Shane*/1953, *Battle Cry*/1955, *Stagecoach*/1966, *Airport*/1970.)

Holbrook, Hal

Drafted in 1943 and served in Corps of Engineers. Stationed in Newfoundland during war. (Films: *The Great White Hope*/1970, *Magnum Force*/1973, *All the President's Men*/1976, *The Kidnapping of the President*/1980, *Wall Street*/1987, *The Firm*/1993.)

Holloway, Sterling

Drafted into the Army during World War II, he was medically discharged after being kicked by a horse. (Films: *The Lavender Hill Mob*/1951, *In Harm's Way*/1964.)

Huston, John

Served two years in the cavalry of the Mexican army and reached the rank of lieutenant before resigning commission at the age of twenty-one in 1928. Subsequently became a screenwriter, actor, and prominent film director in Hollywood. With the advent of World War II, Huston enlisted in the Army Signal Corps in 1942 and was commissioned a lieutenant and assigned to produce propaganda films. He later flew on B-24 Liberators, recording air combat in the northern Pacific. Before being discharged from the Army in 1945, Major Huston produced three of the most realistic documentaries of the war. For his courageous work under combat conditions in both the Pacific and the European theaters, he was awarded the Legion of Merit. (Films: as actor, *The Storm*/1930, *The Cardinal*/1963, *Myra Breckinridge*/1970, *Chinatown*/1974; as director, *The Maltese Falcon*/1941, *Across the Pacific*/1942, *The Treasure of the Sierra Madre*/1948, *Key Largo*/1948, *The Asphalt Jungle*/1950, *The Red Badge of Courage*/1951, *The*

African Queen/1951, *Moby Dick*/1956, *The Misfits*/1961, *The Night of the Iguana*/1964, *Casino Royale*/1967, *The Life and Times of Judge Roy Bean*/1972, *Annie*/1982, *Prizzi's Honor*/1985.)

Ives, Burl

Drafted in April 1942. Made stage debut as singer in Irving Berlin's musical *This Is the Army*. Also had own radio show, *G.I. Jive*, which was broadcast overseas. Given medical discharge in October 1943 after touring with *This Is the Army* but continued to entertain soldiers by making recordings for the Office of War Information. (Films: *East of Eden*/1954, *The Big Country*/1958, *Cat on a Hot Tin Roof*/1958; TV: *O. K. Crackerby*/1965–66, *The Bold Ones*/1969–72.)

Janssen, David

Served during Korean War, 1952–54. Assigned to Special Services at Fort Ord, California. Died suddenly in 1980 at age forty-nine. (Films: *To Hell and Back*/1955, *Lafayette Escadrille*/1958, *The Green Berets*/1968, *Shoes of the Fisherman*/1968, *Inchon*/1982; TV: starred in popular series *Richard Diamond, Private Detective*/1957–60, *The Fugitive*/1963–67, *O'Hara, U.S. Treasury*/1971–72, *Harry O*/1974–76.)

Jones, James Earl

Called to active duty during the Korean War following schooling at the University of Michigan and enrollment in ROTC. First posted to Fort Benning, Georgia, as war was winding down. Ordered to cold weather training in Colorado before discharge in 1955. (Films: *Dr. Strangelove*/ 1964, *The Great White Hope*/1970, *Star Wars* [voice only]/1977, *Conan the Barbarian*/1982, *Coming to America*/1988, *Field of Dreams*/1989, *The Hunt for Red October*/1990, *Patriot Games*/1992, *Clear and Present Danger*/1994, *Cry the Beloved Country*/1995; TV: starred in miniseries *Roots: The Next Generation*/1979, *Gabriel's Fire*/1990–91.)

Kasznar, Kurt

First U.S. Army photographer to film Hiroshima and Nagasaki after the atom bomb was dropped ending World War II. His unit was one of the few chosen to shoot the Japanese surrender on board battleship *Missouri* in Tokyo Bay on 9 September 1945. (Films: *My Sister Eileen*/ 1955, *Casino Royale*/1966.)

Keaton, Buster

Served in France during World War I. Valued as troop entertainer and saw no combat. (Films: *Limelight*/1952, *A Funny Thing Happened on the Way to the Forum*/1966.)

Kelley, DeForest

Served as "Culver City Commando" in Army Air Force film unit during World War II. Loaned to the Navy to work on a film, in which he played a part. Paramount Studios offered him a contract as a result, thus initiating his movie career. (Films: *Man in the Grey Flannel Suit*/1956, *Star Trek* [and sequels]/1979; TV: *Star Trek* series/1966–69.)

Kelly, Jack

Inducted in 1945 and served as weather observer for Army Air Force. Discharged in 1946. (Films: *Submarine Command*/1951, *To Hell and Back*/1956; TV: *Maverick*/1957–62.)

Kennedy, Arthur

Enlisted in the Army Air Force in 1943. Served as corporal during three-year hitch and spent war making training films as part of "Culver City Commandos," the First Army Air Force Motion Picture Unit. Appeared as pilot in training films for P-51 fighter and B-17 bomber aircraft. (Films: *Bright Victory*/1951, *Some Came Running*/1958.)

Kennedy, George

Enlisted at age seventeen and saw combat as infantry soldier in Europe during World War II. Served under Gen. George S. Patton and was awarded two Bronze Stars. Left the Army after sixteen years and became technical adviser to *The Phil Silvers Show*. Bit parts on the television comedy led to eventual acting career. (Films: *McHale's Navy*/ 1964, *The Sons of Katie Elder*/1965, *The Dirty Dozen*/1967, *Cool*

Hand Luke/1967, *Airport*/1970, *Thunderbolt and Lightfoot*/1974, *The Eiger Sanction*/1975, *The Delta Force*/1986, *The Naked Gun 2½*/1991; TV: *The Phil Silvers Show*/1955–58.)

Klemperer, Werner

Served three years in the Army during World War II. Born in Germany in 1920, he came to America with his father, famed conductor Otto Klemperer, after the Nazis came to power. Broke into movies in the 1950s and played character roles, often appearing as bald, monocled Nazi. (Films: *Judgment at Nuremberg*/1961, *Ship of Fools*/1965; TV: best remembered for role as camp commandant, Colonel Klink, in popular series *Hogan's Heroes*/1965–71, for which he won two Emmys.)

Kristofferson, Kris

Son of Army general, became helicopter pilot/Ranger/paratrooper assigned to aviation unit in Germany during Vietnam War. Wrote music in the service and performed at post camps. Taught English at West Point. (Films: *Pat Garrett and Billy the Kid*/1973, *Blume in Love*/1973, *Alice Doesn't Live Here Anymore*/1974, *A Star Is Born*/1976, *Semi-Tough*/1977, *Convoy*/1978, *Stagecoach*/1986, *Cheatin' Hearts*/1993, *Fire Down Below*/1997.)

Ladd, Alan

Inducted into the Army in 1943 and assigned to make training and propaganda films. Medically discharged in November of the same year. Did not see overseas duty. (Films: *Hold 'Em Navy*/1937, *Come On Leathernecks*/1938, *Rulers of the Sea*/1939, *Citizen Kane*/1941, *O.S.S.*/1946, *The Blue Dahlia*/1946, *The Great Gatsby*/1949, *Shane*/1953, *Boy on a Dolphin*/1957, *The Carpetbaggers*/1964.)

Lanza, Mario

Served shortly after close of World War II and was assigned to Special Services. Appeared in Army Air Force musical *Winged Victory*. Possessed a powerful singing voice, and his recordings and movies in the 1950s brought him great popularity. (Films: *Toast of New Orleans*/1950, *The Great Caruso*/1951.)

Long, Richard

Spent two years as a private in Special Services in Japan during Korean War. (Films: *The Dark Mirror*/1946, *The All American*/1953; TV: featured regularly on shows such as *Maverick*/1957–62, *77 Sunset Strip*/1958–64, and *The Big Valley*/1965–69.)

MacRae, Gordon

Trained as Army Air Force navigator/bombardier. Did not leave States during World War II. Following discharge became popular singing star in Hollywood musicals of 1950s. (Films: *The West Point Story*/1950, *About Face*/1952, *By the Light of the Silvery Moon*/1953, *Oklahoma*/1955, *Carousel*/1956.)

Malden, Karl

Served in the Army Air Force from 1943 to 1945. Took basic training at Camp Upton, New York, and performed in service musical *Winged Victory*. Suspected to have tuberculosis and spent a number of months at Fitzsimmons Army Hospital in Denver. Malady turned out to be a lung abscess, which drained and healed itself. (Films: *On the Waterfront*/1954, *One-Eyed Jacks*/1961, *Birdman of Alcatraz*/1962, *Cheyenne Autumn*/1964, *Hotel*/1967, *Patton*/1970; TV: *The Streets of San Francisco*/1972–77. Won Academy Award for best supporting actor in *A Streetcar Named Desire*/1951.)

Matthau, Walter

Enlisted in Army Air Force in 1942 and trained as a radio operator/aviation gunner. Sent to England and assigned to the 453d Bomb Group at RAF station 144, Old Buckham, near Attleborough, as part of Eighth Air Force. Flew several combat missions. Discharged in 1945 as staff sergeant. (Films: *Goodbye Charlie*/1964, *The Fortune Cookie* [won Academy Award for best supporting actor]/1966, *The Odd Couple*/1968, *The Sunshine Boys*/1975, *The Bad News Bears*/1976, *California Suite*/1978, *JFK*/1991, *Grumpy Old Men*/1993.)

McCarthy, Kevin

Served in the Army Air Force from 1942 to 1945. Assigned to Special Services, he performed in AAF musical *Winged Victory*. Brother of author Mary McCarthy. (Films: *The Howling*/1981, *Final Approach*/1991.)

McCoy, Tim

Cowboy movie star who served in both world wars. Part of 88th Infantry Division in World War I, he reached the rank of lieutenant colonel by the end of the conflict. Subsequently settled on large Wyoming ranch that bordered on a Sioux Indian reservation. Became respected expert on Indian culture and dialects. Called to service again during World War II. Duties included teaching Indian sign language to Army intelligence personnel. (Films: *The Thundering Herd*/1925, *The Frontiersman*/1927, *The Overland Telegraph*/1929, *The Westerner*/1935, *Around the World in 80 Days*/1956, *Requiem for a Gunfighter*/1965.)

Meredith, Burgess

Drafted in 1942 and initially stationed at Santa Ana Army Air Force Base in California. Commissioned the same year, assigned to intelligence in the Air Force Transport Command, and sent to England. Discharged in 1944 at the direction of President Roosevelt to play the role of renowned war correspondent Ernie Pyle in the 1945 film *The Story of GI Joe*. (Films: *Advise and Consent*/1962, *Hurry Sundown*/1967, *The Day of the Locust*/1975, *Rocky* [and four sequels]/1976, *Grumpy Old Men*/1993; TV: played the Penguin in *Batman* series/1966–68. Won Emmy for portrayal of lawyer Joseph Welch in docudrama about Senator Joseph McCarthy, *Tail Gunner Joe*/1977.)

Merrill, Gary

Served during World War II from 1941 to 1945 and assigned to Special Services. Appeared in Army Air Force musical *Winged Victory* and Army show *This Is the Army*. (Films: *All About Eve*/1950, *Twelve O'Clock High*/1950, *Navy Wife*/1956, *The Pleasure of His Company*/1961, *The Incident*/1967, *Huckleberry Finn*/1974.) Married to Bette Davis from 1950 to 1960.

Milland, Ray

Native of Wales, he served as a guardsman with the Royal Household Cavalry in London, 1926–29. Relocated in 1930 to America and Hollywood to enhance acting career. Originally cast in supporting roles but later graduated to leads. Tried to enlist in Army Air Force at onset of World War II but rejected because of impaired left hand. Became a civilian flight instructor for the Army and completed two tours of duty in the Solomon Islands in the Pacific. (Films: *Beau Geste*/1939, *The Lost Weekend* [won Academy Award for best actor]/1945, *The Big Clock*/1948, *Dial M for Murder*/1954, *Love Story*/1970, *Battlestar Gallactica*/1979.)

Milner, Martin

Inducted in 1952 and served two years directing series of training films. During tour he was detached from duty for six weeks to play in 1955 movie *The Long Gray Line*, starring Tyrone Power and Maureen O'Hara. (Films: *Pete Kelly's Blues*/1955, *Valley of the Dolls*/1967; TV: *Route 66*/1960–64.)

Mitchell, Cameron

Served in Army Air Force as bombardier during World War II. (Films: *They Were Expendable*/1945, *How to Marry a Millionaire*/ 1953, *No Down Payment*/1957, *Rebel Rousers*/1970, *Easy Kill*/1991; TV: starred in series, *The High Chaparral*/1967–71.)

Mitchum, Robert

Drafted in 1945. Spent eight months as a private at Fort MacArthur and Camp Roberts, both in California, where he became a drill instructor. Received a hardship discharge, claiming six dependents. (Films: *Thirty Seconds Over Toyko*/1944, *The Story of GI Joe*/1945, *The Red Pony*/1949, *River of No Return*/1955, *The Night of the Hunter*/1955, *Ryan's Daughter*/1970, *The Friends of Eddie Coyle*/1973, *Midway*/ 1976; TV: star of popular miniseries, *Winds of War*/1983 and *War and Remembrance*/1988–89.)

Mix, Tom

Cowboy star was inducted at the age of eighteen on 25 April 1898, the day the Spanish-American War began. Assignments included Battery M, 4th Regiment, U.S. Army Artillery, and a coastal artillery unit at Battery Point, Delaware. The following year he was transferred to Battery O at Fort Monroe, Virginia, later relocated to New York and then New Jersey. Sergeant Mix was discharged on 26 April 1901, but reenlisted following day and subsequently married a Virginia schoolteacher. Went AWOL in October 1902 and later listed as a deserter. Never apprehended or taken into custody. (Films: *The Lone Star Ranger*/1923, *Riders of the Purple Sage*/1925, *Destry Rides Again*/1932, *Rustler's Roundup*/1933.) One of most influential figures in rise of western movie genre.

Moore, Clayton

Worked as a "Culver City Commando" in Army Air Force film unit during World War II. Appeared as radar operator in B-29 bomber training films. Was the Lone Ranger in both film and television. (Films: *Kit Carson*/1940, *The Lone Ranger*/1956, *The Ghost of Zorro*/1959; TV: *The Lone Ranger*/1949–52, 1954–57.)

Mostel, Samuel (Zero)

An established comedian in show business, he was drafted in March 1943. Requested position of entertainment director with Army Special Services. Suspected of being a leftist, he was investigated and cleared by military intelligence but nevertheless found not qualified for the position and subsequently given an honorable discharge in August 1943. Discharge papers stated he was released for unspecified physical disabilities. Despite that treatment, he later joined USO groups entertaining troops overseas. Called to appear before House Un-American Activities Committee in 1950s and blacklisted, which nearly ended his career. (Films: *A Funny Thing Happened on the Way to the Forum*/1966, *The Producers*/1968, *The Great Bank Robbery*/1970. He won Tony Awards for Broadway performances in *Rhinoceros* and *Fiddler on the Roof*.)

Nelson, Barry

Served in Special Services during World War II. Appeared in Army Air Force musical *Winged Victory*. (Films: *Bataan*/1943, *Airport*/1970; TV: *The Hunter*/1952, *My Favorite Husband*/1953–55.)

Nelson, Gene

Actor/dancer who served four years in Army in Special Services during World War II. Spent most of hitch touring fifteen countries in Irving Berlin's show, *This Is the Army*. (Films: *I Wonder Who's Kissing Her Now*/1947, *The Daughter of Rosie O'Grady*/1950.)

Norris, Chuck

Enlisted in U.S. Air Force in August 1958. Served as military policeman and spent a year in Korea, where he earned first-degree black belt in karate and brown belt in judo. Training and testing for these achievements were conducted by Korean masters during off-duty hours in Osan. Discharged in August 1962. (Films: *Return of the Dragon*/1973, *Code of Silence*/1985, *Firewalker*/1986, *The Delta Force*/1986, *Hitman*/1991; TV: star of *Walker, Texas Ranger*/1993– .)

O'Brien, Edmond

Enlisted during World War II; served in Army Air Force Special Services and performed in service musical *Winged Victory*. (Films: *The Barefoot Contessa* [won Academy Award for best supporting actor]/ 1954, *Up Periscope*/1959, *Birdman of Alcatraz*/1962, *The Longest Day*/1962, *Seven Days in May*/1964.)

O'Connor, Donald

Inducted in 1944. Served two years and appeared in numerous Army shows. Gifted song-and-dance comedian who began his career on vaudeville stage with his family in his infancy. Made film debut at age eleven and had already appeared in numerous movies prior to induction. (Films: *Beau Geste*/1939, *Francis the Talking Mule* [and five sequels]/1950, *Singin' in the Rain*/1952, *There's No Business Like Show Business*/1954, *Toys*/1992; TV: *The Donald O'Connor Show*/1951 and 1954–55.)

Palance, Jack

Enlisted in Army Air Force in April 1942 and called to duty the following August as an aviation cadet. After twenty-two weeks of training at air bases in Texas, Missouri, and Kansas, he was ordered to

Davis-Monthan Air Base near Tucson, Arizona, where he entered pilot training in B-24 bombers as a second lieutenant. In November 1943 one of his outboard engines quit, the plane crashed, and he suffered severe, disfiguring head and face injuries. Hospitalized for two months and received a medical disability discharge in April 1944. (Films: *Halls of Montezuma*/1950, *Shane*/1953, *The Professionals*/1966, *Oklahoma Crude*/1973, *Bagdad Cafe*/1988, *Batman*/1989, *City Slickers* [won Oscar as best supporting actor]/1991.)

Preston, Robert

Enlisted in 1942. Stationed in England as captain in Intelligence for Ninth Army Air Force. Planned mission routes and briefed and debriefed combat air crews. Discharged in 1945. (Films: *Union Pacific*/1939, *Beau Geste*/1939, *Wake Island*/1943, *The Music Man*/1962, *Mame*/1974, *Semi-Tough*/1977, *Victor/Victoria*/1982.)

Pryor, Richard

Volunteered in 1958. Basic training at Fort Leonard Wood, Missouri, and Army stint at Udar-Oberstein, Germany. Honorably discharged in 1960. (Films: *Lady Sings the Blues*/1972, *Silver Streak*/1976, *Greased Lightning*/1977, *Stir Crazy*/1980, *Superman III*/1983, *Brewster's Millions*/1985, *Critical Condition*/1987.)

Randall, Tony

Served in Signal Corps, 1942–46, initially as a private and later as first lieutenant. Attended officer candidate school at Fort Monmouth, New Jersey. Spent time before discharge as a courier delivering classified documents in Washington, D.C. (Films: *Will Success Spoil Rock Hunter?*/1957, *Pillow Talk*/1959, *Send Me No Flowers*/1964, *Everything You Always Wanted to Know About Sex*/1972; TV: starred in series *The Odd Couple*/1970–75.)

Raymond, Gene

Commissioned as first lieutenant in Army Air Force and initially flew as observer in B-17 bombers on antisubmarine patrols off Atlantic

Coast. Attended Intelligence School and sent to England and 97th Bomb Group in July 1942. Later assigned as assistant operations officer of 8th Bomber Command. Returned to states in 1943, completed flight training and earned wings, and flew B-17s, B-25s, B-26s, and P-39s. Released from active duty in October 1945. Remained in Air Force Reserve following World War II and awarded command wings upon logging five thousand hours in the air. Retired from reserve as colonel. Flew jet aircraft into South Vietnam in 1967 on high-priority missions and awarded Legion of Merit. (Films: *Flying Down to Rio*/1933, *The Woman in Red*/1935, *Smilin' Through* [opposite real wife, Jeanette MacDonald]/ 1941, *Million Dollar Weekend*/1948, *Hit the Deck*/1955.)

Reeves, George

Served in Army Air Force during World War II. Trained initially as radio operator but eventually assigned to Special Services, where he landed top comedy spot in service musical *Winged Victory*. (Films: *Gone with the Wind*/1939, *Samson and Delilah*/1949, *From Here to Eternity*/1953; TV: star of *Superman* series/1951–57.) Unable to find meaningful and secure work after *Superman*, the actor despaired and committed suicide in 1959.

Reiner, Carl

Enlisted in 1943. Originally ordered to Georgetown University's School of Foreign Service. Transferred to 3117th Signal Battalion in Hawaii, but after acting background became known was transferred to Special Services. Spent eighteen months performing in GI shows in the Pacific theater. Discharged in 1945 as sergeant. (Films: *It's a Mad, Mad, Mad, Mad World*/1963, *The Russians Are Coming! The Russians Are Coming!*/1966, *The Jerk*/1979, *All of Me*/1984; TV: *Your Show of Shows*/1950–54, *Caesar's Hour*/1954–57, *The Dick Van Dyke Show*/ 1961–66.) Has won eight Emmy Awards as a comic writer, producer, director, and actor.

Rowan, Dan

Joined Army Air Force at age nineteen during World War II. Severely injured when his P-40 single-engine fighter was shot down over New

Guinea. Spent remainder of war behind a desk. Served from 1941 to 1945. (Films: *Once upon a Horse*/1957; TV: costarred with Dick Martin in *Laugh In*/1968–72.)

Russell, Harold

Enlisted in February 1942 and underwent parachute and demolition training. While instructing a demolition squad of the 515th Parachute Infantry Regiment of the 13th Airborne Division in June 1944, he suffered an accident that caused the loss of both hands. Subsequently appeared in Signal Corps movie, *Diary of a Sergeant,* which depicted his own accident, recovery, and determination to lead a productive life. The film caught the attention of Samuel Goldwyn and he was cast in the movie *The Best Years of Our Lives* (1946), which won eight Academy Awards. Russell was awarded two Oscars, one for best supporting actor and another for "bringing aid and comfort to disabled veterans through the medium of motion pictures." Russell spent the rest of his life championing the cause of the handicapped.

Scott, Gordon

Served at the close of World War II as infantry drill instructor and military policeman. Discharged in 1947. (Films: *Tarzan the Magnificent*/ 1960 [and numerous Tarzan sequels], *Thunder of Battle*/1963.)

Segal, George

Drafted in 1956 and stationed at Staten Island, New York. Discharged with rank of corporal in 1957. (Films: *Ship of Fools*/1965, *Who's Afraid of Virginia Woolf?* [Oscar nomination as best supporting actor]/1966, *A Touch of Class*/1973, *Look Who's Talking*/1989; TV: *Murphy's Law*/1988–89, *Just Shoot Me*/1997– .)

Skelton, Red

Inducted in March 1944. Initially assigned to field artillery, was later ordered to special duty as entertainer on troopships. Discharged in September 1945. (Films: *Whistling in the Dark*/1941, *Ziegfield Follies*/ 1946, *The Clown*/1953, *Around the World in Eighty Days*/1956,

Those Magnificent Men in Their Flying Machines/1965; TV: *The Red Skelton Show*/1951–71.)

Stevens, Craig

Served as a "Culver City Commando" making training and propaganda films during World War II. (Films: *Dive Bomber*/1941, *Since You Went Away*/1944, *S.O.B.*/1981; TV: *Peter Gunn*/1959–63.)

Stone, Lewis

Served in Spanish-American War and won a commission as lieutenant. Participated in World War I as a major. At end of World War I he went to China to train Chinese troops but stay was cut short by Boxer Rebellion. Organized evacuation regiment on West Coast during World War II as lieutenant colonel in California National Guard. (Films: *The Lost World*/1925, *All the Brothers Were Valiant*/1953.) Best remembered for portrayal of Mickey Rooney's father, Judge Hardy, in Andy Hardy film series of 1930s and 1940s.

Taylor, Don

Served in Army Air Force Special Services during World War II and appeared in service musical *Winged Victory*. (Films: *Stalag 17*/1953, *I'll Cry Tomorrow*/1955.)

Torn, Rip

Served two-year hitch during Korean War as military policeman. (Films: *Pork Chop Hill*/1959, *Sweet Bird of Youth*/1963, *Payday*/1973, *Cross Creek* [Oscar nomination as best supporting actor]/1983, *The Hunt for Red October*/1990; *Wonder Boys*/2000; TV: costar of *The Larry Sanders Show*/1991– .)

Wallach, Eli

Served as Medical Services Corps officer during World War II. Discharged as captain at end of war. (Films: *Baby Doll*/1956, *The Magnificent Seven*/1960, *The Misfits*/1961, *The Good, the Bad, and the Ugly*/1966, *The Godfather Part III*/1990; TV: active doing commercial voice-overs and acting in numerous made-for-television movies and miniseries.)

Webb, Jack

Joined Army Air Force in 1943 and trained at Camp St. Cloud in Minnesota. Flew B-26 Marauders before receiving dependency discharge in 1945. (Films: *Sunset Boulevard*/1950, *You're in the Navy Now*/1951, *The D.I.*/1957; TV: best known as star of radio and television series *Dragnet*/1951–59 and 1967–70.)

Wilder, Gene

Served at the Neuropsychiatric Ward of the Army's Valley Forge Hospital in Pennsylvania, 1956–58. (Films: *Willy Wonka and the Chocolate Factory*/1971, *Blazing Saddles*/1973, *Young Frankenstein*/1974, *Silver Streak*/1976, *The Frisco Kid*/1979, *The Woman in Red*/1984.)

Zimbalist, Efrem, Jr.

Enlisted in April 1941 and served as infantry officer during World War II. Was wounded and awarded Purple Heart Medal. (Films: *By Love Possessed*/1961, *Wait Until Dark*/1967; TV: starred in two series, *77 Sunset Strip*/1958–63 and *The F.B.I.*/1965–73.)

Martha Raye

M any today remember actress and comedienne Martha Raye as one of America's favorite entertainers. Others know her best as a stalwart, untiring supporter of the U.S. military. Born Margaret Teresa Yvonne O'Reed on 27 August 1916 in Butte, Montana, she had joined her parents' vaudeville act by the age of three. She appeared in her first feature film, *Rhythm on the Range* starring Bing Crosby, in 1936. The zany comedienne enlivened films and the stage for many years. She possessed a huge, elastic mouth coupled with a highly charged theatrical personality. She was a dynamic entertainer, and her antics both on and off the stage became legendary. She also was a superb singer who could belt out an upbeat tune or enrapture an audience with a romantic ballad.

(Photofest)

In addition to appearing in movies (twenty-six in all, the last being *The Concorde—Airport '79*), she worked in nightclubs, theater, and on television, where she hosted her own weekly program, *The Martha Raye Show* (1955–56). In 1967 she appeared on Broadway, replacing actress Ginger Rogers in *Hello Dolly*. Five years later she was given the lead in the theatrical revival of *No No Nanette*. Raye was married seven times and had one child, Melodye, by husband Nick Condos.

In October 1942 Martha Raye joined actresses Kay Francis and Carole Landis, along with dancer Mitzi Mayfair, in Ireland and England to entertain Allied troops at numerous military bases. During their first six weeks overseas they gave three shows a day, six days a week. They then headed for North Africa on board a B-17 bomber, which was attacked by German fighters over the Bay of Biscay. The aircraft survived, but its tail gunner was killed during the encounter.

Martha Raye, actress and comedienne, was one of America's most popular stars of radio, movies, and television during her illustrious career. Entertaining American servicemen, however, became a serious avocation for her. She spent months overseas entertaining troops during World War II and in Korea and Vietnam. She is shown here with U.S. soldiers in Casablanca, North Africa, in 1943. (National Archives)

When their tour in North Africa ended, three of the entertainers returned to the States, but Maggie (as Raye became known to all) stayed behind to continue giving one-woman shows to the boys on the front lines, frequently traveling by jeep. In addition to entertaining, she could often be seen working with the medics, offering whatever assistance she could. She frequently said that she would like to have been a nurse had she not gone into show business. Suffering from exhaustion from her nonstop schedule, she contracted yellow fever and spent eight days in a military hospital. Once recovered, she was right back in front of the troops, often in remote areas and during Nazi air raids. Maggie returned to New York in 1943, where she proudly displayed an honorary captain's insignia she had been awarded for bravery. She became the first woman designated an honorary captain in the U.S. Army.

That first taste of adulation from military audiences and her heartfelt affection for "her boys" hooked Maggie. For the rest of her life she dedicated herself to them.

In 1952 Raye trekked to South Korea to bring cheer to American fighting men who were up against invading North Korean forces. Unfortunately, she became ill and had to cut her tour short within a few weeks. In just that short time, however, she had endeared herself to the men and women she encountered. Nurses recalled how she visited the wounded and helped them forget their pain by gently talking with them, soothing them, and invariably leaving them with smiles on their faces. Never forgetting the "boys," Maggie headed for Thule, Greenland, in 1954, where she entertained U.S. Air Force servicemen stationed in that remote part of the world.

Maggie's greatest service, however, came when America went to war in Vietnam. In 1965 she traveled to Manila in the Philippines to entertain Navy and Air Force personnel stationed there. She then flew to South Vietnam, where she appeared at numerous bases and outposts. Her promise to deliver letters to families and to telephone loved ones once she got back to the States endeared her to another generation of soldiers fighting a ferocious war. Upon her return she made good her promises and vowed to again visit her "family," as she often called America's military in Vietnam.

Raye went back to Vietnam in the fall of 1965 for a three-month tour; this time she scheduled visits to Special Forces camps and outposts, often playing to as few as a dozen soldiers. In January 1966 she returned home, sporting a U.S. Army Special Forces green beret that had been presented to her. Maggie was often seen wearing jungle fatigues, combat boots, and her green beret in Los Angeles and Hollywood.

The following year she was back in Vietnam in the Mekong Delta when the enemy attacked in force. Maggie hurried to the Soc Trang dispensary to help doctors and nurses care for the incoming casualties. She carried litters, cleaned and bandaged wounds, and gave comfort to those who were giving so much. She openly criticized stateside protesters and American celebrities who traveled to Hanoi to give what she considered aid and comfort to an enemy killing Americans.

Upon her return to the United States, she was cast in the leading role of *Hello Dolly,* a part previously played on Broadway by Carol Channing and Ginger Rogers. She was replaced six months later by Betty Grable because she was set on going back to Vietnam. There, with a small road troupe from *Hello Dolly,* Raye collapsed on stage from heat stroke during the initial show. Yet after a two-day rest she rejoined the players and continued to perform for another two months.

In late September 1967 Maggie and two of her fellow entertainers made an unscheduled stop at a mountaintop outpost. The mountain was called the Black Widow, and its base was controlled by the Vietcong. As she and the others began to perform, the enemy opened up with artillery. A large helicopter that was being used to carry troops answered an emergency call from the soldiers under siege to pick up some VIPs. Raye and her group were quickly evacuated. Earlier that same year President Johnson had named her an honorary lieutenant colonel in the Green Berets, declaring that she was "the first person outside the elite corps (Berets) who may wear their proud symbol." She had also been made an honorary U.S. Army nurse. Maggie traveled to Vietnam again in October 1968 for her own four-month tour. By now she had been named national vice president of a POW-MIA organization. When she went to Vietnam in the fall of 1969, she took part in paratrooper training and made five qualified jumps. She was determined to be a real part of the Army Special Forces.

For her tireless overseas entertainment of America's fighting men, Martha Raye won numerous awards, among them the Distinguished Service Award from the Women's Forum on National Security, the USO Board of Governors Special Award for Gallantry, a Screen Actors

The Vietnam War was to become Martha Raye's obsession. During the war she was frequently seen in-country visiting with troopers in remote, often dangerous, combat areas. Many thought she was a nurse because she spent so much time at base dispensaries, helping to carry litters, cleaning and bandaging wounds, and soothing soldiers with words of comfort and hope. She particularly became endeared to the Green Berets. In order to become a real part of the elite unit, she underwent paratrooper training, making five qualified jumps. President Johnson made her an honorary Green Beret lieutenant colonel. Lt. Col. Maggie Raye salutes troops passing in review during a Veterans of Foreign Wars celebration in New York in April 1967. (Photofest)

Award "in honor of her thirty years of performing for American troops," and the Academy of Motion Pictures Arts and Sciences Jean Hersholt Humanitarian Award "for her devoted and often dangerous work in entertaining troops in combat areas almost continuously since World War II." In October 1993 President Clinton awarded her the Presidential Medal of Freedom.

In January 1990 Maggie suffered the first of several strokes and was diagnosed with Alzheimer's disease. She was in and out of hospitals for several years, and on 19 October 1994 she died at the age of seventy-eight. Because of the honorary rank she held in the Green Berets and her years of service to America's fighting men and women, Martha Raye was honored as the only civilian to be buried in the Green Beret military cemetery at Fort Bragg, North Carolina.

Bob Hope once said of her that "she was Florence Nightingale, Dear Abbey, and the only singer who could be heard over the artillery fire."

Boosting GI Morale

Paulette Goddard was the first actress to visit the China-Burma-India theater. She performed in 130 shows in the area, accompanied by actors Keenan Wynn, William Gargan, and Andy Arcari. (From the book *Movie Lot to Beachhead* [1945] by the editors of *Look* magazine)

Pfc. Eddie Fisher accompanied by an Army band sings for the personnel of the 179th Infantry Regiment, 45th Infantry Division, in Korea, 1952. (National Archives)

Actress Merle Oberon poses for Cpl. Charles Savage as his buddies look on in China, 1941. (National Archives)

Comedian Jerry Colonna of the Bob Hope troupe entertains GIs in Hollandia, Dutch New Guinea, on 2 May 1944. (National Archives)

Famed French entertainer Maurice Chevalier sings in an Allied service club in Paris in 1945. (National Archives)

Actress Jennifer Jones signs her autograph for Cpl. Benjamin Green of Yonkers, New York, at a Mobile Army Surgical Hospital in Korea, 25 May 1951. (National Archives)

Debbie Reynolds, *foreground,* MGM motion picture star and member of a Johnny Grant USO camp show, at the Armed Forces Stadium in Taipei, Taiwan, after entertaining Chinese Nationalist troops and American military personnel in May 1955. (National Archives)

Comedian Joe E. Brown comes on stage to give a show for GIs in China in 1944. (National Archives)

Lily Pons, renowned coloratura soprano of the Metropolitan Opera Company; her husband, conductor Andre Kostelanetz, *standing to her right*; and other entertainers and military personnel take time from their work to visit the West Mountain Temples in China, 28 January 1945. (National Archives)

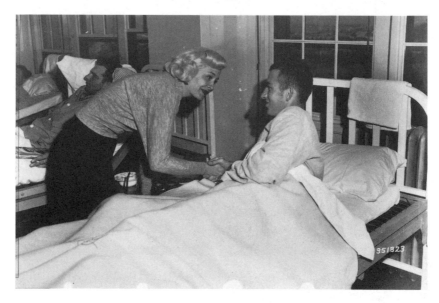

Actress Marilyn Maxwell cheers up Pfc. Raymond Malone of Phoenix, Arizona, at the military hospital in Fukuoka, Japan, 1950. (National Archives)

Singer Dinah Shore entertains GIs in France, 1944. (National Archives)

Actress Marlene Dietrich visits with Army WACS in France, 1944. (National Archives)

Actor Jimmy Cagney entertaining GIs in England, 1944. (National Archives)

Entertainer Bob Hope and his troupe mix with GIs in England. Singer Frances Langford is shown at upper right, 1943. (National Archives)

Movie actor Pat O'Brien chats with Gen. Joseph W. Stilwell, commanding general of the AAF in the China-Burma-India theater, at the general's quarters in China. O'Brien and his troupe were guests of General Stilwell during part of their visit to China, 21 October 1944. (National Archives)

Composer Irving Berlin playing in the WAC mess hall, Hollandia, Dutch New Guinea, 1944. (National Archives)

Actress Ann Sheridan proudly displays a captured Japanese flag in Burma, 1944. (National Archives)

Actress Rosalind Russell is greeted by WACs prior to performing at a stateside camp. (National Archives)

Singer-actor Al Jolson entertains GIs in England, 1943. (National Archives)

Maj. Richard Bong, AAF, the leading American ace of all time, credited with shooting down forty Japanese aircraft, is pictured with, *right to left*, actor Van Johnson, actress Lucille Ball, Mrs. Bong, two unidentified individuals, and actor Keenan Wynn sitting in front. Bong flew a P-38 Lightning fighter, which he christened Marge after his wife. Awarded the Congressional Medal of Honor by Gen. Douglas MacArthur, he was killed while test flying a P-80 jet fighter on 6 August 1945, the same day the atomic bomb was dropped on Hiroshima. (U.S. Air Force)

British actor Leslie Howard, who played Ashley Wilkes in the 1939 film classic *Gone with the Wind*, chats with AAF officers in England. He was lost while flying as a passenger in a British Overseas Airways flight en route from Algiers to London. The plane was shot down by German fighters over the Bay of Biscay in June 1943. (National Archives)

Actress Jinx Faulkenburg plays a game of table tennis with a GI after her show at a forward B-29 base in Chang Tu, China, 9 November 1944. (National Archives)

Twenty-six Hollywood motion picture actors and actresses arrive at Tokyo International Airport en route to entertain UN forces serving in Korea, 25 December 1952. Included in the group are Paul Douglas, Jan Sterling, Joan Leslie, Debbie Reynolds, Carleton Carpenter, and Rory Calhoun. (National Archives)

Johnny Grant, who is known as the film capital's ceremonial mayor, has organized hundreds of visits, many sponsored by the USO, by top Hollywood talent to military installations and veterans hospitals overseas and in the United States He produced Hollywood's Welcome Home Desert Storm Parade, with more than a million people lining the streets to greet returning troops. Here Johnny clearly has troops in Vietnam in stitches. (Johnny Grant)

Those Who Could Not Serve

Many prominent movie stars were unable to qualify for active military duty during World War II because of age, physical impairment, and a variety of other reasons. They were most often classified 4-F (Unfit for Military Service). Although they could not join their fellow Americans in fighting the United States' enemies, many of these celebrities played a large role in boosting the morale of both service members and civilians through their appearances at bond rallies and USO camp shows at home and overseas, as well as through volunteering in USO canteens. Among those who were not able to serve were:

Dana Andrews	Impaired back
Fred Astaire	Too old, married with three children
Jess Barker	Heart murmur
William Bendix	Asthma
Jack Benny	Too old, WWI veteran
Humphrey Bogart	Too old, WWI veteran
Marlon Brando	High school football injury
James Cagney	Too old
Jack Carson	Heart murmur
Montgomery Clift	Intestinal disorder
Steve Cochran	Heart murmur
Ronald Colman	Too old, wounded in WWI
Gary Cooper	Too old, displaced hip following auto accident
Dan Duryea	Heart ailment
Errol Flynn	Heart murmur, tuberculosis
John Garfield	Heart murmur

Cary Grant	Became U.S. citizen in June 1943; not drafted because of report that he had worked for British Intelligence; classified 1-H
Dick Haymes	Hypertension
Bob Hope	Along with Bing Crosby was offered a commission as a lieutenant commander in the Navy. FDR would not allow either to enter any service because he wanted them to entertain all the services.
Van Johnson	Serious skull fracture suffered in auto accident
Danny Kaye	Impaired back
Peter Lawford	Arm injury from childhood accident
Dean Martin	Hernia
Ray Milland	Impaired left hand; served as civilian flight instructor
Gregory Peck	Ruptured vertebrae
George Raft	Too old
Edward G. Robinson	Too old
Cliff Robertson	Eyesight impairment
George Sanders	Pacifist
Phil Silvers	Eyesight impairment
Frank Sinatra	Punctured eardrum; married with children
Pat O'Brien	Too old, WWI veteran
Spencer Tracy	Too old, WWI veteran
Sonny Tufts	Impaired knee
David Wayne	Eyesight impairment
John Wayne	Too old, married with four children, impaired shoulder
Orson Welles	Back impairment
Richard Widmark	Perforated eardrum

Bibliography

Books and Periodicals

Adler, Bill, and Jeffrey Feinman. *Mel Brooks: The Irreverent Funnyman.* Chicago: Playboy Press, 1976.

Agoratus, Steven. "Clark Gable in the Eighth Air Force." *Air Power History* (Spring 1999): 4–18.

Allen, Steve. *Mark It and Strike It: An Autobiography.* New York: Holt, Rinehart and Winston, 1960.

Allen, Thomas B., and Norman Polmar. *Code-Name Downfall.* New York: Simon and Schuster, 1995.

Ambrose, Stephen E. *Citizen Soldiers.* New York: Simon and Schuster, 1997.

Audie Murphy Research Foundation Newsletter. Vols. 1–7, Winter 1997–Spring 1999. Santa Clarita, California.

Autry, Gene. *Back in the Saddle Again.* Garden City, N.Y.: Doubleday, 1978.

Baron, Scott. *They Also Served.* Spartanburg, S.C.: MIE Publishing, 1998.

Bean, Orson. *Too Much Is Not Enough.* Secaucus, N.J.: Lyle Stuart, 1988.

Bennett, Tony. *The Good Life.* New York: Pocket Books, 1998.

Bonderoff, Jason. *Alan Alda: An Unauthorized Biography.* New York: New American Library, 1982.

Bowman, Martin W. *USAAF Handbook 1939–1945.* Mechanicsburg, Pa.: Stackpole Books, 1997.

Chant, Christopher, consultant ed. *Warfare and the Third Reich: The Rise and Fall of Hitler's Armed Forces.* New York: Smithmark Publishers, 1996.

Clark, Alan. *Aces High: The War in the Air over the Western Front 1914–18.* New York: Barnes and Noble Books, 1999.

Cohen, Stan. *V for Victory: America's Home Front During World War II.* Missoula, Mont.: Pictorial Histories Publishing, 1991.

Current Biography Yearbook. New York: H. W. Wilson, 1940–98.

Davis, Ossie, and Ruby Dee. *With Ossie and Ruby: In This Life Together.* New York: William Morrow, 1998.

Davis, Sammy, Jr., Burt Boyar, and Jane Boyar. *Why Me? The Sammy Davis, Jr. Story.* New York: Farrar, Straus and Giroux, 1989.

Dictionary of American Biography, Supplement Nine, 1971–1975. New York: Scribner's Sons, 1975.

Dorr, Robert F. *B-24 Liberator Units of the Pacific War.* Oxford: Osprey Publishing, 1999.

Douglas, Helen Gahagan. *A Full Life.* New York: Doubleday, 1982.

Editors of Look. *Movie Lot to Beachhead.* New York: Doubleday, Doran, 1945.

Fisher, Eddie. *Been There, Done That.* New York: St. Martin's, 1999.

———. *Eddie: My Life, My Loves.* New York: Harper and Row, 1981.

Fishgall, Gary. *Against Type: The Biography of Burt Lancaster.* New York: Scribner's, 1995.

Foster, Col. Frank, and Lawrence Borts. *U.S. Military Medals: 1939 to Present.* Fountain Inn, S.C.: Medals of America Press, 1998.

Freeman, Don. "Back in the Saddle Again: Television's No. 1 recluse, James Arness, comes out of hiding for another Western." *TV Guide,* 1977, 3–16.

"Friendly Fire Key to Miller Mystery?" *Coloradan,* August 1999, 3.

Graham, Don. *No Name on the Bullet: A Biography of Audie Murphy.* New York: Viking, 1989.

Gunston, Bill. *Jane's Fighting Aircraft of World War II.* London: Jane's Publishing, 1991.

Guralnick, Peter. *Careless Love: The Unmaking of Elvis Presley.* New York: Little, Brown, 1999.

Hall, James Norman, and Charles Bernard Nordhoff. *Lafayette Flying Corps.* New York: Houghton Mifflin, 1920.

Harris, Warren G. *Lucy & Desi.* New York: Simon and Schuster, 1991.

Heller, Jonathan, ed. *War and Conflict: Selected Images from the National Archives, 1765–1970.* Washington, D.C.: National Archives and Records Administration, 1990.

Heston, Charlton. *In the Arena: An Autobiography.* New York: Simon and Schuster, 1995.

———. "The President's Column: Taking a Stand for the Second Amendment." *American Rifleman,* January 1999, 12.

Heston, Charlton, and Jean-Pierre Isbouts. *Charlton Heston's Hollywood: 50 Years in American Film.* New York: CT Publishing, 1998.

Heyn, Howard C. "Elephant Boy, Now a Flying Gunner Home on Furlough." *Hollywood Citizen News,* 31 July 1945.

Hobson, Dick. "He Never Loses His Cool." (On Jack Warden.) *TV Guide,* March 1966, 15–20.

Hoopes, Roy. *When the Stars Went to War: Hollywood and World War II.* New York: Random House, 1994.

Jarvis, Everett. *Final Curtain: Deaths of Noted Movie and Television Personalities.* Secaucus, N.J.: Carol Publishing Group, 1998.

Johnsen, Frederick A. *Consolidated B-24 Liberator.* Vol. 1. North Branch, Minn.: Specialty Press Publishers and Wholesalers, 1996.

Jordan, René. *Clark Gable.* New York: Pyramid Publications, 1973.

Kaplan, Mike, ed. *Variety: Who's Who in Show Business,* rev. ed. New York: Garland Publishing, 1985.

Katz, Ephraim. *The Film Encyclopedia.* New York: Harper Perennial, 1998.

Kesselring, Albert. *The Memoirs of Field-Marshal Kesselring.* London: Greenhill Books, 1997.

Knutzen, Elrik. "Jack Warden Still Has His Spirit of Adventure." *Los Angeles Herald Examiner,* 30 December 1984.

Lambert, Bruce. "Neville Brand, 71, Craggy Actor Known for Many Roles as Villains." *New York Times,* 19 April 1992.

Latham, Caroline, and Jeannie Sakol. *E Is for Elvis: An A-to-Z Illustrated Guide to the King of Rock and Roll.* Harmondsworth, England: Penguin Books, 1991.

Leibfred, Philip. "Sabu." *Films in Review,* October 1989, 451–57.

Lewis, Kevin. "The Two Careers of Melvyn Douglas." *Films in Review,* October 1981, 453–67.

Malden, Karl. *When Do I Start?* New York: Simon and Schuster, 1997.

Maltin, Leonard. *Leonard Maltin's Movie Encyclopedia.* New York: Penguin Books, 1995.

———. *1999 Movie and Video Guide.* New York: Penguin Books, 1999.

Martin, Mick, and Marsha Porter. *Video Movie Guide 1998.* New York: Ballantine Books, 1998.

Maurer, Maurer, ed. *Combat Squadrons of the Air Force in World War II.* Washington, D.C.: USAF Historical Division, Air University, 1969.

McCombs, Don, and Fred L. Worth. *World War II: Strange Fascinating Facts.* New York: Greenwich House, 1983.

McNeil, Alex. *Total Television.* New York: Penguin Books, 1984.

Meredith, Burgess. *So Far, So Good.* New York: Little, Brown, 1994.

Morison, Samuel Eliot. *History of United States Naval Operations in World War II.* 15 vols. Boston: Little, Brown, 1947–62.

Moser, Don. *World War II: China-Burma-India.* Alexandria, Va.: Time-Life Books, 1978.

Murphy, Audie. *To Hell and Back.* Blue Ridge Summit, Pa.: Tab Books, 1949.

Newton, Michael, and Roger Sabin. *The Movie Book.* London: Phaidon Press, 1999.

Norris, Chuck, with Joe Hyams. *The Secret of Inner Strength: My Story.* New York: Charter Books, 1988.

"Oklahomans to Observe Tim Holt Day September 13." *Boxoffice,* 28 July 1975.

Parish, James Robert. *Hollywood Character Actors.* New York: Arlington House Publishers, 1978.

"Personality & War Film—Colonel James Stewart." *After the Battle* 1 (1973).

"Personality & War Film—Lieutenant Audie Murphy." *After the Battle* 3 (1973).

"Personality & War Film—Major Clark Gable." *After the Battle* 11 (1976).

"Personality & War Film—Major Glenn Miller." *After the Battle* 2 (1973).

Pisano, Dominick, Thomas J. Dietz, Joanne M. Gernstein, and Karl S. Schneide. *Legend, Memory and the Great War in the Air.* Washington, D.C.: Smithsonian Institution Press, 1992.

"Playboy Interview: James Garner." *Playboy,* March 1981.

Poitier, Sidney. *This Life.* London: Hodder and Stoughton, 1980.

Potter, E. B. *Sea Power: A Naval History.* Annapolis: Naval Institute Press, 1981.

Pryor, Richard, with Todd Gold. *Pryor Convictions and Other Life Sentences.* New York: Pantheon Books, 1995.

Quinlan, David. *Quinlan's Illustrated Directory of Film Stars.* New York: Hippocrene Books, 1986.

Rader, Dotson. "An Actor Deals with His Darker Side." (On Richard Pryor.) *Parade,* 10 October 1993.

Randall, Tony. *Which Reminds Me.* New York: Delacorte Press, 1989.

Reagan, Ronald. *An American Life*. New York: Simon and Schuster, 1990.

Rooney, Mickey. *Life Is Too Short*. New York: Villard Books, 1991.

Schickel, Richard. *Clint Eastwood: A Biography*. New York: Vintage Books, 1997.

Simon, George T. *Glenn Miller and His Orchestra*. New York: Thomas Y. Crowell, 1974.

Slawson, Judith. *Robert Duvall: Hollywood Maverick*. New York: St. Martin's, 1985.

Starr, Michael Seth. *Art Carney: A Biography*. New York: Fromm International Publishing, 1997.

"Stars' Names to Cover Tim Holt Grave in Oklahoma." *Boxoffice*, 15 September 1975.

Taggart, Donald G., ed. *History of the Third Infantry Division in World War II*. Nashville: Battery Press, 1987.

Thomas, Bob. *Golden Boy: The Untold Story of William Holden*. New York: St. Martin's, 1983.

Thomas, Tony. *James Stewart: A Wonderful Life*. New York: Carol Publishing Group, 1988.

Tornabene, Lyn. *Long Live the King: A Biography of Clark Gable*. New York: G. P. Putnam's Sons, 1976.

Troth, Riley. "Miller Mystery." *Coloradan*, December 1999, 21.

U.S. Army Studies. *The U.S. Army Campaigns of World War II* pamphlets: *Rome-Arno; Naples-Foggia; Southern France; Normandy; Central Burma; Burma, 1942; India-Burma; China Offensive; Aleutian Islands*. Washington, D.C.: Government Printing Office, 1972.

Vandour, Cyril. "Holt and Sons." *Photoplay*, November 1942, 89–90.

Van Osdol, William R. *Famous Americans in World War II*. St. Paul, Minn.: Phalanx Publishing, 1994.

The Variety Insider: Editors of Variety. New York: Berkley Publishing, 1999.

Walker, John. *Halliwell's Filmgoer's Companion*. 12th ed. New York: Harper-Perennial, 1997.

Wheal, Elizabeth-Anne, and Stephen Pope. *The Dictionary of the First World War*. New York: St. Martin's, 1995.

Wheal, Elizabeth-Anne, Stephen Pope, and James Taylor. *Encyclopedia of the Second World War*. Secaucus, N.J.: Castle Books, 1989.

Wilkinson, Philip, ed. "Hollywood's Greatest Legends: Clint Eastwood." *Star*, 21 July 1998, 20–22.

Wright, Michael, ed. *The World at Arms: The Reader's Digest Illustrated History of World War II*. New York: Reader's Digest Association, 1989.

Official Records and Archival Sources

The below listed official sources were used in compiling data for this book. Material used included official documents; unit histories/historical studies; biographical information; citations; press releases; photos of movie stars who served in the U.S. Army, U.S. Army Air Force, and U.S. Air Force; and miscellaneous reports.

Center of Military History, Fort McNair, Washington, D.C.

Department of the Army, Review Boards Agency, Arlington, Virginia.

Library of Congress, Washington, D.C.

National Archives, College Park, Maryland.

National Personnel Records Center, St. Louis, Missouri. Unfortunately most of the service records for World War II U.S. Army and Army Air Forces personnel were destroyed in a 1973 fire at the center. A few records were reconstructed from other center documents, but where center records proved invaluable for *Stars in Blue* and *Stars in the Corps*, little could be found of use in *Stars in Khaki*.

U.S. Air Force 90th Space Wing, F. E. Warren Air Force Base, Cheyenne, Wyoming.

U.S. Air Force Historical Research Agency, Maxwell Air Force Base, Alabama.

U.S. Air Force Museum Research Division, Wright-Patterson Air Force Base, Dayton, Ohio

U.S. Army Military History Institute, Carlisle, Pennsylvania.

Other Sources

Academy of Motion Picture Arts and Sciences Library, Los Angeles. Biographical and other information about many actors, including James Arness (Metro-Goldwyn-Mayer Studios biography, c. 1955), Neville Brand (United Artists Studios biography, 1962), Melvyn Douglas (Paramount Studios biography, 1963), Tim Holt (RKO Radio Pictures Release biography, 1948), Jack Warden (Warner Brothers–Seven Arts Studios biography, 1967), and Muriel Davidson, "Unlikely Brothers: James Arness and Peter Graves."

Audie Murphy Research Foundation, Santa Clarita, California. "Complete Description of Service Rendered" statements by Company B, Fifteenth Infantry soldiers in support of Medal of Honor for Audie Murphy: Sgt. Elmer C. Brawley, USA; Pfc. Anthony V. Abramski, USA; Staff Sgt. Norman O. Hollen, USA; Lt. Col. Keith L. Ware, USA; and various related high-level endorsements recommending award. "Official Statement of Military Service of Audie Leon Murphy, 01 692 509 Certified by Adjutant General of the U.S. Army. Audie L. Murphy Medal Award Citations: Medal of Honor, Distinguished Service Cross, Silver Star (1st Oak Leaf Cluster), Legion of Merit, Bronze Star (1st Oak Leaf Cluster), Purple Heart (1st and 2d Oak Leaf Clusters)." Washington, D.C.: Department of the Army, Office of the Adjutant General, 1945. "Listing of Foreign Decorations Awarded Audie Murphy." Washington, D.C.: Department of the Army, Office of the Adjutant General, 1945.

Autry Museum of Western Heritage, Los Angeles.

Butcher, Geoffrey. Liner notes for *Glenn Miller: The Lost Recordings*. BMG Music, 1995.

Elvis: King of Entertainment. New York: Good Times Home Video Corporation, 1997. Videocassette.

Margaret Herrick Library, Center for Motion Picture Study, Academy of Motion Picture Arts and Sciences, Academy Foundation, Beverly Hills.

"Melvyn Douglas." Biographical Information printed by Paramount Studios, 1963.

Ronald Reagan: The Role of a Lifetime. Arts and Entertainment (A&E), 1996. Videocassette.

Variety Obituaries. Vols. 1–15. New York: Garland Publishing, 1905–94.

Index

About the Authors

James E. Wise, Jr., became a naval aviator in 1953 following graduation from Northwestern University. He served as an intelligence officer aboard USS *America* (CVA-66) and later as the commanding officer of various naval intelligence units.

Since his retirement from the Navy in 1975 as a captain, Wise has held several senior executive posts in private sector companies. In addition to *Stars in Blue: Movie Actors in America's Sea Services* and *Stars in the Corps: Movie Actors in the United States Marines,* he is the co-author with Otto Giese of *Shooting the War: The Memoir and Photographs of a U-Boat Officer in World War II.* He is also the author of many articles published in naval and maritime journals. He lives in Alexandria, Virginia.

Paul W. Wilderson III is executive editor at the Naval Institute Press. He holds a Ph.D. in American history and is the author of a biography of John Wentworth, the last royal governor of New Hampshire. Wilderson's articles and reviews have appeared in *The Journal of American History, American Quarterly,* the *Boston Globe, Historical New Hampshire,* and the *American National Biography.* He lives in Stevensville, Maryland.

The **Naval Institute Press** is the book-publishing arm of the U.S. Naval Institute, a private, nonprofit, membership society for sea service professionals and others who share an interest in naval and maritime affairs. Established in 1873 at the U.S. Naval Academy in Annapolis, Maryland, where its offices remain today, the Naval Institute has members worldwide.

Members of the Naval Institute support the education programs of the society and receive the influential monthly magazine *Proceedings* and discounts on fine nautical prints and on ship and aircraft photos. They also have access to the transcripts of the Institute's Oral History Program and get discounted admission to any of the Institute-sponsored seminars offered around the country.

The Naval Institute also publishes *Naval History* magazine. This colorful bimonthly is filled with entertaining and thought-provoking articles, first-person reminiscences, and dramatic art and photography. Members receive a discount on *Naval History* subscriptions.

The Naval Institute's book-publishing program, begun in 1898 with basic guides to naval practices, has broadened its scope in recent years to include books of more general interest. Now the Naval Institute Press publishes about one hundred titles each year, ranging from how-to books on boating and navigation to battle histories, biographies, ship and aircraft guides, and novels. Institute members receive discounts of 20 to 50 percent on the Press's more than eight hundred books in print.

Full-time students are eligible for special half-price membership rates. Life memberships are also available.

For a free catalog describing Naval Institute Press books currently available, and for further information about subscribing to *Naval History* magazine or about joining the U.S. Naval Institute, please write to:

Membership Department
U.S. Naval Institute
291 Wood Road
Annapolis, MD 21402-5034
Telephone: (800) 233-8764
Fax: (410) 269-7940
Web address: www.usni.org